Behavioral Marketing

Behavioral Marketing

Delivering Personalized Experiences at Scale

Dave Walters

Library of Congress Cataloging-in-Publication Data:

Walters, Dave, 1968-
  Behavioral marketing : delivering personalized experiences at scale / Dave Walters.
      pages cm
  Includes index.
    ISBN 978-1-119-07657-5 (hardback) – ISBN 978-1-119-07639-1 (ebk) –
ISBN 978-1-119-07643-8 (ebk)   1. Internet marketing.   2. Customer
relations.   3. Consumers' preferences. I.   Title.
  HF5415.1265.W3655 2015
  658.8'72–dc23
                                                        2015017698

Printed in the United States of America

10 9 8 7 6 5 4 3 2 1

CONTENTS

FOREWORD

There is a customer revolution underway.

Buyers today have more information, more access, and more choice than anytime in history. The battleground for customer loyalty has shifted from features, prices, and transactions toward the new landscape of long-term relationships and customer experience. Best-in-class companies like Apple and Lexus have rewritten the rules of customer relationships by leveraging every touch point and every interaction to create a convenient, fun, and even meaningful experience. They have embraced the customer revolution, and they are raising the bar for the rest of us.

Marketing has always been the bridge that connects businesses and customers. However, marketing needs to reinvent itself in this new world of customer experience, moving beyond its roots in the audience/content/publish cycle. The new generation of marketers needs to embrace every customer interaction, digital or offline, no matter how diverse or seemingly short lived. We need to engage with each customer when and where that customer prefers with content that is perfectly tuned and individualized to him or her.

We can expect that, in return, customers will not only make purchases; they will offer their attention, their time, and their loyalty. To make this transition, we marketers must move beyond the day-to-day mechanics of campaign execution and curating content. We have to embrace our origins as storytellers and pull ourselves forward to become the architects of customer experience.

Imagine that marketing is like touring a city. Most of today's marketing does little more than crowd tourists into a small set of the most popular destinations. More advanced marketing is like a tour bus that is taking tourists to more destinations with smaller crowds. However, the sequence is fixed and the experience still fairly generic.

The future of marketing is like having your own private concierge who knows your interests, your budget, and your pace. This guide walks alongside you delivering a completely unique and personal experience perfectly tailored to you.

In the same way, the future of marketing will be built around each customer's unique personal interests. And like an experienced tour guide, marketers learn a customer's interests by asking what they want. But the truly world class tour guides go beyond asking; they watch their customer's behaviors as they visit each leg of their tour to craft a truly epic journey and experience the customer will never forget.

Marketers will be the architects of customer experience, and behavioral marketing will provide the foundation and write the guide book that marketers use to construct and orchestrate **epic** customer experiences.

But first, a little history . . .

My first small steps on the journey toward behavioral marketing took place in 2004. At the time, I had just released a book called *The Quiet Revolution in Email Marketing*. I wrote the book to help marketers recognize email marketing's ability to go beyond its roots as a "batch and blast" interruptive advertising channel.

I defined the world of email marketing in three levels, the first being basic personalization. Back then, well over 10 years ago, a large portion of email marketing wasn't even personalizing first names, so Level 1 was a big conceptual step for many marketers. Level 2 led marketers into the world of audiences, segmentation, and customers' stated preferences. And Level 3, the most advanced marketing at that time, pushed marketers into dynamic content, lifecycle campaigns, and analytics for creating even more relevant segments and targets.

In the last section of the *The Quiet Revolution in Email Marketing*, I hinted at a world beyond Level 3 that we are just now embracing 10 years later: that we would be segmenting customers by their past behaviors and even responding to those behaviors in real time. For many marketers, including Silverpop and me, this was the first time the idea of behavioral marketing had surfaced.

But as it turned out, those words would lead to the core vision and strategy that transformed Silverpop beyond email marketing and into one of the earliest pioneers of behavioral marketing and customer experience.

In 2006, our business was thriving. Email marketing was one of the hottest growth areas for marketers. So it surprised Silverpop's board of directors somewhat when I approached them with the idea that winning in email marketing might not be winning at all. Even back then, email marketing was starting to be overdone. It had been so successful for marketers that inboxes were getting flooded and buyers and customers were turning away from the channel. I told the board that it was the ideal time for us to evolve and cast a more differentiated vision.

We spent the following few quarters seeking out the next big thing. We looked at mobile, content management, and even deeper analytics, but along the way, we stumbled into what became a central part of our future: business-to-business (B2B) marketing automation. As our strategy thinkers were looking into their long-term crystal balls, our sales team was looking for some practical, near-term solutions to better manage leads.

They had found a small set of software providers that sat on top of our sales automation and customer relationship management (CRM) platform to help capture and nurture leads. As the sales execs were reviewing the vendor options, we all realized that the email marketing was at the heart of these new B2B marketing automation solutions and that it was something we should probably do ourselves.

It ended up taking us a long time, with more than a few false starts. But in the end we acquired one of the leading B2B vendors, Vtrenz, and used their expertise to create the platform that ultimately redefined our company and even the marketplace: Engage 8. This revolutionary solution was the world's first marketing platform to combine the individual customer journeys of B2B marketing with the incredible scale and content control of business-to-customer (B2C) email marketing.

As Engage 8 hit the market, everyone agreed that we had developed something truly unique. For the first time, marketers could create individualized dialogs with millions of customers, one at a time, in real time. To be honest, it took a year or two for our customers—and even Silverpop itself—to realize the potential of what we had created.

I will never forget the comment made by one of our larger CPG (consumer packaged goods) customers who themselves offered dozens of highly complex customer journeys across email, social websites, and their website: "Silverpop is the best email marketing company in the world." Although clearly flattering, it also reminded me that the true potential of our platform was still tied to its reputational roots as a channel-specific delivery tool.

It was time for us to take a bold stand and—like the college student who realized he had picked the wrong subjects—to declare a new major. We needed to focus our energies on behavioral marketing and the true future of the marketing profession: customer experience.

In the years following, behavioral marketing was the center of attention at Silverpop. We created features like progressive profiling, send-time-optimization and, the most important of all, our technology to support any kind of customer activity or behavior in real time, which we called universal behaviors. We drank our own champagne and relaunched Silverpop.com. Our website became one of the most powerful examples of behavioral marketing; as buyers and customers traversed the site, we learned what they were interested in and changed the content to reflect it. Visitors' behaviors also drove and influenced the content we sent them in newsletters. All this was powered by our vision of behavioral marketing and running natively on our Engage 8 platform.

When IBM acquired our company in May of 2014, they cited our behavioral platform and application programming interfaces (APIs) as some of the most compelling reasons to work with us. And now, as part of one of the largest technology companies in the world, we are yet again reinventing what it means to create epic customer experiences.

The future of marketing is being rewritten, and for marketers across the world, there has never been a better time to be in our profession.

The customer revolution that is well underway is about each individual customer having an experience uniquely tailored to his or her needs, interests, and expectations. Audiences, segments, and targets are not going away, but the future of marketing relationships is personal and will reflect and respect each customer's individuality.

Marketers need to interact with customers based on their behaviors. This goes beyond clicks and page visits to include interactions like visiting physical stores, achieving fitness goals, calling customer support, reaching new levels in games, using new product features, installing mobile apps, trialing a software tool, walking by a museum exhibit, posting social comments, reading a blog, and countless others.

Marketers cannot interact with individual customers in batches. But reacting in real time to customer behaviors is just the start. We must also curate content into unique stories for each customer. Analytics must uncover each customer's expectations, preferences, and intent. Ultimately, marketers must define road maps that allow customers to navigate their own unique path at their own pace toward a wide set of individual destinations.

I have had the privilege of working with Dave Walters for over a decade, first as one of Silverpop's most visionary clients and more recently as one of Silverpop's most prolific thought leaders and influencers. The moment he approached me with his idea of a book on behavioral marketing and buyer experiences, I knew he was the right person to translate Silverpop's unique experiences into a story to be shared with marketers across the world. I cannot begin to measure all that I have learned from working with Dave over these many years. I hope each of you reading his book is able to gain as much from his perspective and experiences as I have.

—Bill Nussey

CEO, Silverpop, an IBM Company

ACKNOWLEDGMENTS

First, my wife, who more than holds down the fort while I'm off meeting with marketing teams around the world. She's our True North. And my two daughters, ages seven and five, who only ask Daddy for fun gifts from Melbourne, Australia not Melbourne, Florida. Without all my girls I would lack an understanding of life, love, and the world.

Professionally, those who have formed my views of marketing and technology for the last 20 years, including Hugh MacLeod, Gary Vaynerchuk, Chris Brogan, Rand Fishkin, Mark Suster, Brad Feld, Tom Tunguz, and Tim Ferris. They think deeply, challenge the norms, share with the world at-scale, and have been responsible for educating a generation of marketers and startup types. We collectively owe them a debt of gratitude that can be repaid by sharing their thinking across social networks and buying their books. The *Hughtrain Manifesto,* the *Thank You Economy* and everything ever written on Tom Tunguz's blog could easily be a master-class-in-a-box for digital marketing.

Finally, to my friends and colleagues at Silverpop—particularly Bill Nussey and Bryan Brown—it has been a joy to be part of the journey to move marketing beyond batch-and-blast to behavior-powered interactions. We started as a strong independent company with more than a decade of marketing tech innovation, and our latest journey as part of IBM's Commerce Group will supercharge our ability to help marketers be more successful and fulfilled in their roles. Here's to another decade of innovation.

And I'll end with my favorite Hugh MacLeod cartoon of all time, which reminds us to keep our marketing thinking human-powered and massively relevant to the individual.

IF YOU TALKED TO PEOPLE THE WAY ADVERTISING TALKED TO PEOPLE, THEY'D PUNCH YOU IN THE FACE.

©hugh

THE BEHAVIORAL MARKETING MANIFESTO

When we talk about how industries change and when new thinking emerges, the concept of a manifesto is one that surfaces often. Whether you're a fan of religious figures like Martin Luther and his 95 theses or your thinking leans more toward the business world's Cluetrain Manifesto, outlining a core set of truths can be a powerful way to set the frame of reference for the next phase of the conversation.

Given that this is the first deep-dive book on behavioral marketing, I thought it'd be valuable to outline 50 of the top-line theories in a quick format that sets the concepts for the rest of the chapters. I've broken the manifesto into 10 key sections ranging from marketing to team to revenue. Think of these as guiding principles, and we'll dive into each of them in much more detail throughout the book. And yes, they're tailor-made for social sharing, should the urge strike you.

Marketing

1. Almost every sale begins with marketing. Get it right, then scale.
2. Marketing is your best chance to frame the buying decision in your favor. Start early.
3. Marketing without a point of view is time and money wasted.
4. There's a human on the other end of every marketing experience. Recognize that.
5. Understand the difference between the science and art of marketing. Be better at both.

Sales

6. A marketer's best friend is a well-informed sales rep.

7. Expect CRM drama between sales and marketing. Solve it with more qualified leads.

8. Sales complains about logging activity, until they close six more deals a month.

9. Sales is comp-driven first, but don't underestimate the roles of team and mission.

10. Done well, great sales informs better marketing—and vice versa.

Customer

11. Your customers will solve their business problems—with or without you.

12. Cherish your existing customer base and build raving fans from day one.

13. Your goal: remain so critical your customers don't even accept competitor calls.

14. Build a core competency in customer listening—and do it closest to your most progressive executive.

15. Your customer's skill set is a broad spectrum: some are at ground zero, some are improving fast, some could teach you.

Prospect

16. Educating prospects is marketing's most important job. Always and forever.

17. If you don't positively articulate your value proposition, your competitors will stack the deck against you.

18. Winning content strategy is built on value exchange. You provide insight, they share data and let you keep competing.

19. Understand the lead source, content-consumption preferences, and behaviors of your best prospects and double down.

20. Choose the best three social destinations for your prospects and engage like your business life depends on it. It does.

Data

21. Data driven is nice, but conversion driven is better.

22. Care more about what your audiences do than what they say.

23. It's marketing's job to figure out how to make sense of all that data. Start now and work it hard.

24. All the data in the world won't gloss over bad customer experience or poor campaign execution.

25. Customer data is like human knowledge—build it from diverse sources over a lifetime with specific goals in mind.

Behaviors

26. One "buy now" button click is worth 100 email opens.

27. Buyer intent is captured in actions, not in words. Sales and marketing should both understand this reality.

28. Behaviors are a marketer's treasure map, defining the path to conversion moments.

29. A great scoring model includes behaviors, demographics, sentiment, and complete objectivity.

30. Factoring your customer experiences for behavior transforms marketing effort into revenue.

Team

31. Hire for potential, and be prepared to mentor your staff to greatness.

32. Build a team and culture that incents and celebrates new-hire referrals from existing employees.

33. Require your marketers to work directly with sales management on program development and reporting.

34. Hire an expert on your marketing platform of choice. Their deep skill enables your success.

35. Develop a strong competency around hiring brilliant 25-year-olds. They're tomorrow's directors and VPs in training.

Company

36. It's your job to educate your executives on marketing. Ignore this at your own peril.

37. Your company has a story. Discover it and anchor your marketing on its principles.

38. No one cares about the constraints you work under. Give 120 percent to every customer experience you tackle.

39. Authenticity and trust are the basis of every great customer relationship.

40. Look beyond your industry for winning marketing tactics. Different is better.

Vendors

41. Trust but verify in the demo phase. Evaluate on end-to-end solutions, not slide ware.

42. Outsource when necessary, but develop your own policies and processes to drive execution.

43. Use agencies to scale your most successful marketing programs while challenging them to develop big ideas.

44. Clearly understand and enforce how your vendors work together to make your marketing better.

45. Cheaper isn't always better. Hire the best thinking your budget can buy, and track ROI like a beast.

Revenue

46. Revenue lift cures almost all ills.

47. If you're ignoring behaviors today, you're missing a huge chunk of income—especially in ecommerce.

48. Every marketing interaction costs money. Being brutally efficient on cost drives top-line revenue.

49. Great marketing makes your customer want to give you money. Don't get in the way.

50. Email open, customer satisfaction, and hold-time key performance indicators (KPIs) are important. Revenue trumps them all.

Part One
Getting Started With Behavioral Marketing

1 Behavioral Marketing

More Sophisticated Audiences, Smarter Tactics, and Deeper Personalization for All

If you've read this book's foreword (and you definitely should), then you should already have a good idea of the big picture of the market's needs and wants. Put simply, marketing is an ever-evolving discipline—and the latest iterations of that change are powering sales lift and better customer experiences across the entire spectrum.

There's a relatively simple concept behind all this improvement: what someone *does* is critically important in deciding how to reach (and convince) him or her most effectively. Their **behavior**—whether captured during a sales call, or measured at-scale by an activity like a website page visit—represents an incredible moment of insight for the marketer savvy enough to listen closely and act on that information.

Is behavioral marketing the latest fad to wash over the marketing landscape for the next three to four years? The answer is a definite maybe. The customer focus it encourages—and the revenue increase it creates—are the basic underpinnings of epic improvement. So this might be the first title of 1,000 you'll read on the topic.

If it doesn't elevate to fad status, the best outcome ever might be that behavioral marketing simply pervades every corner of traditional marketing. Instead of some overused buzzword that enters the realm of *synergy*, it may well become the lens through which we look at everything. If everyone who reads this book upped their own conversion rates by 10 percentage points, we would push an entire industry ever closer to their customers—which is always a good thing.

Dave Who?

Before you commit to reading this entire book, you'll probably want at least some assurances that your author is qualified on the topic (beyond the Wiley-picks-smart-authors factor). I am aware from personal experience that your time as a marketer is massively precious.

I know exactly how crushed you are at work, and that you have eight cross-channel campaigns in production right now, and more than half have outstanding issues that could kill them before they're ever ready to deploy. If you're an email marketer, you've got a template that you've needed to update to mobile for six months but you can't get a designer to stop working on website enhancements long enough. If you're a CRM professional, your sales and marketing colleagues are probably still bickering about what exactly a sales qualified lead (SQL) is, even though they agreed to a definition six months ago. Regardless of what channel you manage—or if you're the chief marketing officer (CMO) or VP orchestrating the entire effort—you work in a warp-speed, high-wire environment in which the difference between a better subject line or tighter audience segmentation could mean the difference between hitting your revenue goals this quarter—or missing them by 20 percent.

I know so much about the marketing drama because I've spent more than 20 years as a digital marketer. It is literally all I've ever done. Oscillating between the agency and corporate worlds has afforded me a view of the first 25 chapters of the story well enough to know there are at least 25 more. I've had marketing performance and staffing pinned to my shirt long enough for year-over-year metrics to be the true success criteria, and I've had to build new functions and groups out of thin air into productive existence in less than three months.

I've walked the walk inside the halls of huge companies. I was at UPS early in my career as a digital native brought in to scale the competency internally. Most recently, I joined IBM as one of the thought leaders and experts within Silverpop that IBM bought in 2014 to further expand the digital marketing offerings in the IBM Commerce group. I've also consulted with the biggest brands on the planet while working with leading digital agencies like Tribal DDB and Digitas in all areas of marketing including loyalty and retention marketing.

But much of the experience on which I'll base this book is made up of perhaps the coolest aspect of my current job at IBM. I'm what's called an *evangelist*, and my job is to help digital marketers be more successful every single day. I meet with more than 100 marketing groups every year and help solve their biggest challenges. Some days we're very focused on pure marketing tactics that we can accomplish using our technology; but more often it's a larger optimization and orchestration challenge that requires improvement across multiple groups.

I've seen firsthand how the most progressive marketing teams continually reorient themselves around their customers. And the solution that works most often is simply to begin listening more closely to individuals—but also at scale. They pay attention to specific behaviors—sometimes as a stand-alone event, or in combination with other behaviors—and use the information they gather to segment their audiences into smaller and smaller groups. Once those groups are small enough to share major traits like buying propensity, they architect massively relevant communications and offers based on driving the desired outcome.

It's a beautiful thing to watch as a trusted advisor—and this book's goal is to give you the insight necessary to integrate the exact same types of improvement into your own marketing effort. We're going to cover topics far and wide on behavioral marketing—from how to refactor each of your channels to be more behavioral driven down to how to become a Top 5 brand for your customers. We'll go deep on data capture, hygiene, and critical technology pieces needed to win in this emerging world. And we'll spend lots of time talking about staffing, retaining, and motivating a behavioral-marketing-optimized team.

Why Behavioral Marketing?

The basic reasons for thinking deeply about behavioral marketing are pretty straightforward: (1) it increases your orientation toward the customer; and (2) it requires you to think critically about the relevance and trust that each marketing interaction conveys. When we put ourselves in our customer's shoes through exercises like customer journey mapping and user-centered design, we are able to deliver personalized and relevant experiences. And when we orchestrate a great content strategy during the prepurchase process, we're building the trust necessary to close that big deal.

Furthermore, because there's an entire spectrum of how deeply you can accept behavioral marketing into your marketing practice, you can spread your improvements over time and make measured, positive change. I talk all the time with our customers about **scaling change** into their marketing group. Being more behavioral driven doesn't mean you have to re-engineer every marketing practice on one random Tuesday. If you're an ecommerce operation, then figure out how to improve your cart abandon offer strategy while building new browse abandon automated programs. Improve your welcome campaign, but also do some heavy-duty testing of subject lines in the sale messages that go out to your largest audiences. Dialing improvements across all your campaigns will drive very real increases in your top-line revenue numbers.

If you sell products or services directly to businesses, take an honest look at how well you work with sales. Do your nurture programs improve the recipient's understanding of the offering well enough to close more sales? Are you scoring interactions across the behavioral spectrum so you can inform a true funnel, from initial lead source all the way to conversion?

If you're like many marketing groups and have both B2C and B2B in play, then think critically about the best-of-breed tactics you could deploy across all your audiences. Some of the most successful B2B programs I've seen have the personalization and strong visuals that are a hallmark of great consumer campaigns. And one of the most important tactics for building a trusted relationship with a consumer is a prepurchase content strategy that scores and ranks recipients throughout the process—exactly like a B2B marketer executes a traditional nurture program.

The best reason to tackle behavioral marketing is that it's an incredibly scalable way to drive more revenue from your marketing efforts. You only have to make minimal changes to show strong revenue-growth potential that pays off even more as you add additional segmentation strategies and automated programs. You can bite off the concepts at almost any level and drive more sales. I'd encourage every marketer to think of behaviors as the new lens for how you look at your entire marketing effort.

Definitions We Should Cover Upfront

In working your way through this book, we're going to cover many behavioral-marketing-oriented ideas and program types. It's likely worth defining a few of these terms so the least experienced marketers reading this don't have to stop in the middle to Google phrases. If you've been in the game for more than three or four years, you can probably skip this section, but a refresher course might also be in order.

So here's a selection of the key concepts I'll be referring to during the rest of the book:

Audience segmentation: The process of splitting your list into many smaller lists based on secondary criteria such as email opens, purchases, or demographic elements.

Automated programs: A setup-once, run-many-times program that sends one or more messages to users based on their behaviors, time in the program, or other measured variable.

Best-friend brand: The process required to become one of the Top 5 trusted brands in your recipient's inbox.

Browse abandon: An automated program that's often a single step and is based on someone visiting a specific site section or stock-keeping unit (SKU).

Cart abandon: An automated program that normally is three steps (typically something like event +1 hour, +2 days, and +4 days) and based on someone placing an item in an online shopping cart but not purchasing it.

Content strategy: The process of creating presale and postpurchase content (think whitepapers or shoe fitting guides) that provide product or company insights to the recipients, and drive a significant source of customer behaviors for the marketer to measure.

Deliverability: The process of managing the delivery of mass email messaging to your recipients via Internet Services Providers (ISPs) like Google or Hotmail.

Triggered message: A one-time automated message that's not sent as part of a multi-user campaign—think of an e-commerce purchase receipt.

Net Promoter® Score: A scoring model in which you ask your recipients if they'd recommend your product or service to a friend, and the results are scored on a 1 to 10 scale.

Web Tracking: The process of installing a unique JavaScript line of code to a website or app to identify known and anonymous users and track their behaviors. Beyond traditional web analytics, this tracking allows a marketer to build automated programs triggered by onsite behaviors, email-only behaviors, other channel behaviors, or a combination of all three.

Behavioral Marketing Campaigns You've Seen in Everyday Life

The other very clear way to define behavioral marketing is to point to individual campaigns you've seen in your own inbox or customer experiences you've had with your favorite brands. Among the most common pure behavioral-driven email campaigns is the trusty cart abandon program. I'll tell the entire story around this example in Chapter 15, but Figure 1.1 is a great example of cart abandon content. It's 100 percent based on my shopping activity, it's time driven based on when I carted the item, and a subsequent communication had a promotional offer as a last resort to get me to buy. If you sell items via the web, this is almost a must-do tactic.

The other triggered message you'll often see if you use a lot of social networks focuses on building your on-site network. When the site wants you to match an address book contact to your on-site network, there's often a message that looks like the Foursquare one in Figure 1.2—relatively simple and straightforward with a single call to action. Conversely, some apps and brands use triggered email as a means to let you know that one of your contacts (matched from your phone) or your Facebook friends has joined that specific site and you should connect your profiles.

Another non-email version of behavioral marketing you've probably seen involves interactive voice response (IVR) systems at your utility companies—in my case, Comcast. When I dial into the 800 number,

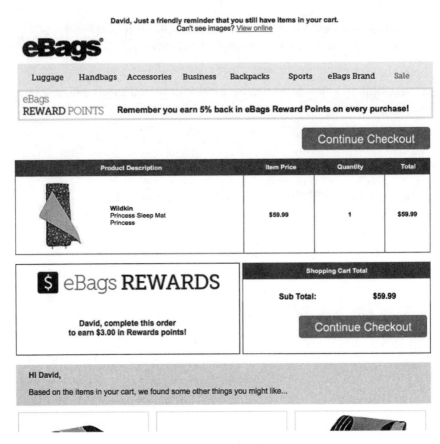

Figure 1.1 Cart Abandon Content

the system automatically recognizes me by name and confirms the last four digits of my phone number on file. It then offers me the next pay-per-view event by simply selecting a number on the keypad. And if I end up talking with a representative, then the process of confirming my identity is simply a matter of confirming my street address.

This takes into account everything Comcast knows about me from an account perspective, offers me a purchase opportunity, and streamlines my customer service event—all in a single, intuitive flow. By surfacing this knowledge directly into the IVR, they speed the entire experience and even have a chance at booking some bonus increase in revenue.

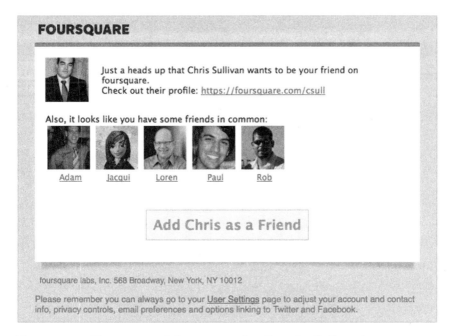

Figure 1.2 Foursquare Message with a Simple Call to Action

And finally, let's look at a completely different behavioral marketing tactic that's wrapped in a financial product. Every time I shop at Target, an employee offers me one of their Target Red debit cards—a card product tied to your bank account just like a traditional bank debit card would be, but with a 5 percent discount on everything in the store. How can they afford to do this? Beyond reinforcing Target as your retailer of choice by seeing that red bulls eye logo every time you open your wallet, there's a critical amount of data flowing over that card.

Their ability to identify you as a unique individual—and track all your purchases over time by department, by time of day, and so forth—allows Target to build incredibly specific, data-driven personas they can act on from a marketing perspective. They might send out four different versions of a flyer—baby items, electronics, home furnishings, and toys—and some percentage of the audience is going to get one of these specialty versions if they have sufficient data to show they belong in that segment. The rest will receive a nonspecialized version of the same flyer.

Interestingly enough, I've never signed up for the Target card because I actually choose my bank based on the fact that they have a debit card product that earns me Delta Sky Miles (this will not surprise you in the least by the time you finish this book). At the same time, I **do** have one from Nordstrom Rack based on the significant value proposition they deliver, including $5 birthday coupons, early access to certain sales, and other benefits like free alterations. I'm willing to exchange the risk of allowing a nonbanking entity link to my bank account in exchange for the solid value proposition they offer. This, by itself, is an excellent behavior that the Nordstrom marketing team can factor into all kinds of audience segmentations they want to turn on.

These examples show that behavioral marketing is all around us every day—and that determining how to integrate it into your marketing approach isn't rocket science. It requires putting yourself in your customer's shoes, and being data driven enough to be able to listen at scale and deliver personalized messages based on what you know.

In fact, I know marketers whose extent of behavioral marketing is to resend every wide-scale email message to the nonopening segment exactly 24 hours after sending the first message, but with a different subject line the second time. If 20 percent of recipients open the first message, then the day-after audience is 80 percent of the original list, and the second version they get (with a new subject line) drives another 8–10 percent of opens that time around.

That's the beginning of an epic behavioral-marketing-driven approach, and if every marketer reading this book looked for one small strategy like that to execute, we'd all be on an awesome improvement path.

Relevance Trumps Privacy under 35—Every. Single. Time.

One of the themes you'll notice throughout the book is the concept of being data driven. This can be a source of concern for marketers, especially as you get into European Union countries with much more restrictive laws, or if you're focusing on a marketer's ability to build a purchase history like the debit cards we discussed earlier can provide. Although there certainly are legal guardrails you need to know and follow—think HIPAA for the healthcare industry (the federal Health Insurance Portability and Accountability Act) or COPPA (Children's Online Privacy Protection Act) for marketing to children under age 13—you should think about your audience as either above or below 35.

If your main audience is under 35, you should pretty much delete the concept of privacy from your vernacular. Although this might sound aggressive, those generations are usually more than comfortable exchanging privacy for a more relevant experience. My Nordstrom debit card is the exact evidence of this phenomenon (although I'm admittedly a couple of years past 35).

However, if you're marketing to AARP-age people, then I recommend almost the opposite. You should ratchet down the obvious manifestation of data-driven communications. Avoid messages like "We saw you stopped by the website." Your audience doesn't give you a pass to ignore behavioral marketing. In fact, you might have to work a little harder to better inform your audience segmentation models and do more behind the scenes.

And if your audience is in the middle age-wise, you should proceed with caution. Think deeply about their motivations, communication preferences, and how other high-profile brands are marketing to them when developing your approach. Keep it mostly low-key—but don't be afraid to be aggressive with dynamic content as the audience segments get progressively smaller.

If you can isolate your ecommerce audience down to those who have spent more than $1,000 at your site over the last six months and they open 80 percent of all your communications, then experiment with highly personalized offers that are clearly focused on "Our Best Customers." Exploring the correlation between behavior and purchases is a great area for marketers to experiment with.

Conclusion

As we get started on this behavioral-marketing journey, I'm going to offer a few hints:

1. Remember you can tackle this at your own pace.

2. Focusing on behaviors makes your marketing more about your customer's needs than it is today.

3. More behavioral marketing equals more revenue or a better-informed recipient in almost every case I've ever seen.

4. Making more money and/or happier customers gets you promoted *fast*.

So keep an open mind and look for ways to improve your current programs. And ask yourself how many new segments you could define within your audience, and how you'd structure a communications strategy for each. These simple first questions based on a broader way of thinking about marketing will lead you in the right direction—and the success you uncover will be the fire that keeps you going.

2 Where Are You on the Behavioral Marketing Spectrum?

If every great journey begins with the first step, then reorienting your marketing thinking around behavioral marketing could be the most important step in the whole process. Many of us are actually behavioral-driven marketers without even realizing it. We naturally select our best customers to receive the best discounts, and we gravitate to retention marketing without having all the metrics in place to prove it's the smarter way to go. By gut feel, I'd suggest that most critical-thinking marketers actually factor for customer behaviors without even knowing they're doing it.

But this chapter doesn't focus on what happens by coincidence or by mistake. Rather, it will provide a series of very clear litmus tests to help you figure out where you are today, what your potential looks like, whether you have the needed technologies, and how complex of a path you'll need to chart to get there.

Defining Your Now

Of all the steps in this—or any—transformation, the first is typically the hardest. That's not because the task is so monumental; it's because you need to break out of a previous way of thinking, regardless of how successful your trusted approach has been. It also takes time and some serious consideration to decide to replace your lens on the world, which is an analogy I don't use flippantly. In order to drive meaningful, long-lasting, epic change in your marketing, you absolutely must change your fundamental outlook. The burning questions is no longer "How big is my list?" It's now, "What's the best offer for that high-value segment?"

You'll hear this many times throughout the book, but now is the moment when you need to clearly understand your business at a very deep level. If we're going to revamp marketing's view of the customer, you'd better have a lot of insight on their needs and wants. You must appreciate fully what you customers want to buy from you—and what they feel would be a stretch for your current brand-level relationship.

For example, many people buy different styles of shoes from radically different retail outlets for lots of reasons. The Mom who defines almost all household-spending dynamics is a study in contrast by herself. She may buy her work and dress shoes from Zappos because of their great customer service and return policies, her kids' shoes from Nordstrom based on immediate availability and wide selection, and her own athletic shoes from a local specialty sporting goods retailer like Modell's or Dick's based on aggressive pricing on her preferred brand. Knowing what she expects from a shoe seller is a complicated matrix of price, availability, brands, and shopping preferences.

To truly understand where you lie today, look at your marketing on two specific axes: today's *success rate* and how *personalized* you are. Said simply, you need to baseline your marketing performance against your direct competitors (or proxies in other industries); and you need to be very honest about how well you communicate with individuals. If your results are middle-of-the-pack in revenue, and all your campaigns are batch-and-blast messages where everyone gets the same message, then you've got some serious work to do—but also, some nice potential upside in your results.

Conversely, if you're a market-leading brand like Nike that excels at personalized messaging based on products owned or known hobbies like running, your effort is going to be more subtle—and may not have a huge immediate upside. You may have to work harder to achieve eye-popping results, but you will already be feeling the benefits of more personalized marketing.

Once you've honestly assessed your current results—and for most a 1 to 10 scale is the most relevant measuring stick—then take an equally critical look at your personalization. Again, assigning yourself a 1 to 10 score is probably a great way to quantify your current and future state. The litmus test here should be how many microsegments are you actively marketing to.

To define this specifically, ask yourself, How often do I send a customized message to a subset of my overall list? For example, give yourself major credit for cart-abandon email campaigns, but subtract a point or two if you blast out a sale email every Thursday. There's certainly a time and place for that sale email, but for the purposes of quantifying your effort, you need to have at least one great behavior-driven email to offset that blasting technique.

So, in essence, you'll end up with a scorecard for your email efforts. Although it might not be something as complex as you'd assemble for your customer-facing efforts, having a quantified measure of your "now" state is an important first step and allows you to measure improvement over time.

Tackling Channels One at a Time

A large portion of this chapter will focus on a single channel: email. It's the most widely used, affordable tactic in most marketers' arsenal. When you're mapping out the implications of behavioral marketing, it's best to initially take a channel-by-channel view, and then build that into an overall score. Because each channel has its own dynamics, it's important we don't confuse the tactics with a channel's natural rules.

For example, your customer support function by definition is going to be highly personalized and dynamic because you're dealing with an individual customer's very specific issues. In this case, your behavioral marketing goals might be more focused on building a killer Net Promoter® Score (NPS®) model into your follow-up process.

It's also important to note that not every marketer is going to tackle every channel. Either you don't have one in play (no brick-and-mortar stores), or you're resource-constrained and can't boil the ocean this year. So thinking about each channel separately and scoring them the same way allows us to aggregate the scores by channel into an overall behavioral marketing quotient.

Building Your Behavioral Marketing Quotient

Although it sounds daunting, the beauty of quantifying the smaller parts of your effort is that you can simply add them together to get the larger score. This is also important in determining how to improve. For example, a marketer might quantify four of the channels (email, direct mail, social, and call center) to arrive at an overall quotient of 24 (assuming they're equally weighted in importance).

Your goal may then be to get to 30 by the end of that calendar year. You can undertake changes in any of the channels, and the individual score improvement will lift the overall quotient. This is especially vital early in the process when there are many gains to be had. Measuring this lift over time by channel is also an important step in quantifying your efforts.

A word of caution: many marketers tend to be oversharers, and they can't help but want to publicize every new method and campaign. This isn't necessarily bad; it's just that the first steps on this journey should probably focus more on self discovery and honest assessments.

Although these scores and quotients might be the type of data a marketing director could use as a construct with their managers and staff, they aren't necessarily the kind of key performance indicators (KPIs) I'd be socializing up to my senior vice president. We'll come back to the topic of managing both up and down your executive chain in the next chapter, but suffice to say you'll want to perfect the methodology and populate a couple of solid quarters of data before you go shouting about it from the proverbial mountaintop.

What About Your Organization?

Although assessing your own channel-level marketing performance is the first (and most important) step, it'd be foolish to ignore the bigger construct in which you'll be working. Having a realistic but aggressive view of your company's readiness to think more about behaviors than traditional marketing tactics is an important baseline to articulate.

I'd suggest you use the same 1 to 10 scoring basis you have used for your channels, and then update that metric over the next two to three years. Give your organization credit for improvements, but also be critical of cutbacks that lead to fewer customer-driven choices and less personalization. You might not know every detail of each corner of the business, but keep a general idea of how things are going.

Although it's important to recognize your company's overall orientation toward behavioral marketing, I'd caution marketers to *rarely* use this as an excuse for not being aggressive in your own programs. Sure, some industries (and specific companies) may have regulations and rules that forbid retaining deep customer information for marketing purposes: for instance, alcohol companies who are prohibited from marketing to under-21 users. But don't fall into the trap of the "this is how we do business" mentality passed down from higher-ups. If this is the case, then it only highlights the upside potential of you bringing this level of thinking to your company.

Technology Is Absolutely Your Friend

There are many ways to reorient a company around behavioral marketing, but one of the most critical moments often involves either new or upgraded technology that comes into the marketer's area of responsibility. Many times, that early-stage email platform your predecessor bought simply runs out of steam as your lists become bigger and your desires become more behavioral. Or maybe you're using a brand-new CRM to more closely orchestrate the customer touchpoints between sales and marketing—an epic moment for any growing company.

The bottom line is that your technology stack is one of your most powerful allies in becoming a true behavioral marketer. If you have deployed a rock-solid marketing automation platform, you can almost manage the entire effort out of the marketing department without relying on others within your company.

If you execute your business more significantly on mobile platforms (think inside an app) than on a traditional website, your analytics software must provide key insights into your customer's mobile behaviors. You must gather data on information such as number of logins, overall session times, task-completion stats, and other key measures related to your specific business. I work with a huge number of businesses whose primary tasks are completed in the mobile app, but who track all the behaviors and activity metrics in the marketing automation platform. This allows them to easily trigger email-based reminders and manage an aggressive re-engagement campaign for users who stop using the app.

Finally, you'll need to take a proactive role in the technology selection process within your marketing and IT functions. If you're a director or vice president, you may be the main stakeholder for any purchasing event, which means that it's your job to articulate the business value, define your requirements, and select vendors. Leaving these tasks to others in your organization—particularly IT—is a recipe for disaster.

Oddly enough, the worst-case scenario is *not* that you have no marketing technology to help you execute. It's normally easier to make a case to license a good software-as-a-service (SaaS) tool for a reasonable cost if you can prove the return on investment (ROI) quickly. Rather, the situation to avoid above all else is getting an overly complicated, difficult-to-use system as part of a larger technology purchase.

I've seen this happen repeatedly for the last 15 years. Normally it's the large-scale enterprise resource planning (ERP) vendors like Oracle or SAP who will throw in a marketing module for little or no cost while the company spends millions on accounting or finance solutions. If you can't operate and enhance the technology stack at the pace marketing requires (which is normally warp speed compared to finance), then you're in a very tough spot. The business can point to this big investment in marketing, but it's difficult to show consistent revenue lift.

This is exactly why you need to be marketing's number-one advocate for highly usable SaaS-based technologies. Spend time getting to know peers in your industry and understand which vendors have rock-solid solutions for your common use cases. And don't think you have the luxury of making too many wrong decisions; you likely have one shot to get the technology stack right or you're going to be one of two things: really frustrated at work or starting a new job.

Conclusion

Overall, the question of behavioral marketing readiness is an incredibly personal topic, and I'd encourage marketers to be as aggressive as possible when painting the future vision. As a group, we're incredibly aspirational and have the capacity to lead the discussion because we're an integral part of the customer and revenue equations. If we as marketers don't lead this conversation, who will? Normally not finance or IT or sales: it truly belongs in the marketing function.

The next chapter of marketing is ready for us to write it. As Bill Nussey emphasizes in the book's Foreword, the world has changed. Our customers expect much more from us than just offering products for sale. They want education. They want postpurchase support. They want discounts. They want brand experiences. It's marketing's job to deliver all this, and leaving the "how" for others to decide is a critical error.

So get out there and start building your internal relationships. Be a vocal advocate for upgrading your marketing technology stack because you clearly understand how much more you'll be able to accomplish with your staff of three. Build ROI cases based on data from industry analysts and comparable customer case studies. Engage and lead these conversations across your organization, and I promise you'll reap the benefits after you execute well.

So now that you have a framework for understanding your current state, the next task is to think through the elements you'll need to build success into your plan. The great behavioral marketers concentrate on three key areas of focus: roles, people, and technology systems. So let's dive in . . .

3 Gearing Up for Behavioral Marketing

The Roles, People, and Systems Needed to Win

Now that you've got a solid idea of where you are, let's look forward to the ideal pieces you need in place to complete the transformation. You'll probably tire of hearing me say that this is a gradual process, but it's a critical point. Very few marketers can make wholesale changes to their practices overnight. Most of us have to continue executing while driving improvement into our processes incrementally. The only scenario I've seen that calls for complete, instantaneous transformation is one in which a new executive is hired into a close-to-death company and radical change is the only way to keep the lights on—and I hope you're not in that spot!

Roles, Job Titles, and Getting Things Done

One of the great things about my role at Silverpop is my opportunity to see the inner workings of at least 100 top-tier marketing groups a year. Some are deeply stacked teams with all resources on a single floor, working together seamlessly; others are small hit teams of two or three killer marketers who are forced to work with creative and IT in a shared-services capacity and hire solid vendors. Since both scenarios can be equally successful, be careful what you wish for in terms of the future state of your group.

Before we dive all the way in, let's look at a perfect example of a small, brilliant team that out-executes many of the bigger teams I see. I work closely with a leading software company that has more than 10 titles marketed to individuals and work groups via the freemium model (where the software is free to try for a period of time or with limited functionality, but after that it requires a subscription to continue its use). In addition to separately marketing each title to those who sign up for the trial, they have an aggressive cross-sell and upsell methodology that helps users understand the benefits of their other tools and how those same benefits apply to other groups within their company. It even includes a by-seat-per-company analysis so they can see when to invoke an enterprise sales rep for an account where more than two groups are using a specific tool.

The average marketer's head might explode just thinking through the upgrade nurture programs required to predictably convert free users to paid users for 10+ software titles. They are apt to wonder what the right cadence is for communication, and what offer converts best (extend-the-trial, one-month-free-with-annual-subscription, etc.)? When we account for time in combination with this nurture process (normally 14 or 30 days industry-wide), we have to extrapolate how many touches work best and what stage in the process is ideal.

Many companies in this spot will have a 14-day trial-to-upgrade program that looks like this:

1. Welcome and thanks for trialing (sent immediately on signup).

2. Product benefits and getting started tutorial (8-12 hours later).

3. Reminder to login (day two if no user login has occurred).

4. More advanced tutorial (day five + three logins).

5. First upgrade offer (day six + three logins).

6. Survey (day 10 + five logins).

7. Second upgrade offer (day 12 + five logins).

8. Expired notice with final offer (day 14 + five logins).

9. First re-engagement (day 18).

10. Final re-engagement (day 20).

If it's 10 touches per trial user and you've got 10 products to support, and your paid media and search actives are optimized well enough to drive 500 trials per weekday across all products—you're talking *serious* volume. There is absolutely no way to be successful in this world without massive automation and a rock-solid technology stack. You *start* a set of nurture streams totaling 5,000 messages every single day that takes into account both time and user actions.

Now what if I told you that a mere **three** people ran that marketing function? I discuss much of what makes them so successful, and why they're the blueprint for great behavioral marketing in the rest of this chapter. I also work though the application for more traditional campaign-based marketing operations and marketing groups of all sizes and compositions.

Let's get back to the roles within your marketing group. Although the structure might differ in hundreds of ways based on your business, internal politics, or how your budget is funded, certain roles are a constant. The typical marketing reporting structure looks like this:

- CMO/SVP: Leads the overall marketing vision, responsible for revenue generation from all marketing activities.

- VP: Typically the reporting focal point for all the channel-based groups, responsible for optimization of channel mix.

- Director: Plans and manages the execution of a specific channel, responsible for maximizing individual channel success metrics.

- Manager: Executes a specific channel, responsible for getting the job done.

- Specialist: Supports the manager with execution, responsible for compiling reports and other admin duties critical to running the group smoothly.

I'm going to leave creative out of the marketing-specific job roles for now—for the simple reason that it's often still a shared service across multiple groups inside a company. For some companies—like Silverpop—the creative function is aligned under its own director and part of the marketing group in reporting structure, but still has external customers across the organization. Regardless of where creative services reports, they're most likely to have customers across the expanse of an organization—from the CEO's office to investor relations to sales operations.

One role I increasingly see in hypersuccessful marketing groups is an analyst-type position that takes on many names. Sometimes it's called a database marketing manager, and there are one or two specialists on the team who focus on data modeling and reporting. Other times, the function is filled with the skills of a certain specialist on the team without naming the role at the director or manager level.

Regardless of what it's called or where it reports, this role is critical in the transformation to behavioral marketing. Typically, the person filling it has some IT-based skills and may have actually come to marketing from that world. As a result, they bring to the group a numbers-driven, data-oriented view of audience selection and the scientific method necessary to drive smart A/B test methodologies and fact-based assumptions. These skills beautifully complement a great artistic, human-powered marketer who can empathize with their audience at a personal and persona level.

When thinking about reorienting your effort around behavioral marketing, it's crucial to understand that it can effectively occur at every level already outlined—from the CMO to the specialist. Of course, your success will be more institutional the higher the thinking rises within the company—but **do not** think that a single manager can't make a huge difference in factoring for customer behaviors.

Let's return to the earlier software company example. In that scenario, the director of marketing leads the behavioral marketing initiative almost completely; all his executives know is that his numbers are "through the roof." Sure they ask some second-order questions about tactics and challenge him to drive his results even further, but they're not in the weeds of audience selection and messaging cadence.

Conversely, I've seen many scenarios in which a new CMO or SVP is hired into a small-to-medium sized company and the tone changes almost immediately. The focus moves from historical methods to the customer. This changes quickly for two significant reasons: budget reallocation and new director hires. Oftentimes, a CMO has at least a couple of trusted colleagues to bring over to the new company, prompting an up-and-down synchronicity of thinking that makes for a powerful method for change. Moving dollars between channels can also be an important signal in expectation setting for the entire marketing department.

You should be mentally prepared for any and all leadership changes in your marketing group, since most will signal an increase in per- formance- and behavioral-based marketing. Sure there are cases in which poser bureaucrat types work their way into roles at their friends' companies to run marketing, but by and large most staffing moves in marketing today reflect the growing importance of the function—both in budgeting and contribution to revenue.

If you're a director or below, you should be plotting to *lead* the revolution—especially if you work in a traditional marketing group with mediocre results, where nothing much has changed in the two years you've been there. Architect a vision and approach that you can achieve in the short-term that features 2–3 quick revenue-driving wins.

Seek the absolute minimum permission needed to make these changes, and get down to business. There are two critical pieces of advice I often share with my customers (and my two young daughters, too) that come from two of my favorite rap artists, Chingy and Lil Wayne, respectively: "Don't talk about it, be about it" and "No sittin' at the table unless you're bringin' something to it."

There may never be a more opportune time for a young marketer to be a catalyst for change. The market is inevitably moving toward more quantified, personalized buying experiences, and building your competency now will pay great dividends for your future and allow you to succeed in your current role. So **be** the change, and don't wait for a new CMO to bring in a new hotshot director—when you knew what to do the whole time.

The Art and the Science of Marketing

One of the other common conversations I have with our customers focuses on the importance of recognizing and celebrating two very different sides of marketing: art and science. For decades, the marketing function has involved a series of incredible artistic moments. Beginning with advertising agency legends such as Leo Burnett through today's great initiatives like Dove's Campaign for Real Beauty, there's no doubt that resonant messaging and the ability to tell a genuine story are hallmarks of effective creative.

Although these large-scale campaigns and messaging platforms will continue to drive business (and awareness) for the biggest brands that can afford the millions of investment dollars required, there's an emerging application for this great creative, but it's in much smaller chunks. The same way these huge firms resonate with broad audiences is the way that effective behavioral marketers think about resonating with small segments. So their genius is applied in much the same way, just in more highly relevant moments.

Therein lies one of the most important points of recognition for anyone on the journey toward behavioral marketing. We can now take in a massive amount of data, understand where our prospects and customers are in the buying cycle, and then serve them the ideal message. We can use our creative brains to model out the critical customer journeys, leverage our scientific methods to track and assess specific events within those journeys, and then circle back to our creative prowess to deliver the most compelling message at the right time.

This is precisely why I see the most effective marketing groups blending the two skills together almost seamlessly. Focusing on one more than the other is not necessarily a gigantic mistake; it only leaves a ton of upside on the cutting room floor. Can you be good at the art but ignore the science? Maybe, but you're likely not going to scale your effort to 10 product lines the way we described earlier. And you're probably always going to need more design help from outside agencies. Can you ignore the art, and be a great data-driven marketer? Sure, but if you can't demonstrate a highly personal understanding of your customers and be a very effective storyteller both visually and with words, they'll eventually find one of your competitors who's more compelling. That's simply the nature of how humans buy things today.

Hiring for Potential

I'm going to spend a minute talking about hiring practices and how to build your team. If things are going well and you're beginning to lead the behavioral marketing revolution inside your company, you're inevitably going to have to make some key additions to your team. This moment of hiring may be the single most important inflection point in your behavioral-marketing growth pattern. You've architected a plan, sold the vision enough to begin execution, gotten early wins, and proven revenue life—but now it's time to scale.

There are an abundance of perspectives on how to hire great marketers—but mine's almost exclusively focused on the idea of potential. Although having a base-level understanding of marketing functions is critical for the lower half of any marketing organization, one of the enemies of success is typically the statement, "That's how we did it at my old company." If I hear that in an interview, my brain tunes out just a tiny bit. What I'm looking for when hiring is someone dripping in constructive dissatisfaction. I want to hear, "I wish my boss would let me . . ." or "We need to spend more time testing . . . ."

This is especially true when hiring managers and specialists. You're typically talking to someone with less than five years experience, and at some level you need to look three years into the future in terms of what kind of marketer you think you can cultivate. As it happens, I've been known to select a candidate for the specialist role based 100 percent on potential. When I worked for UPS, I hired a superbright intern directly from an administrative role and shepherded her through the tuition-reimbursement program to finish her technical college degree—all while working with her to deepen her marketing knowledge. We worked together for many years afterward.

The moral of the story: ignore what degree someone holds, and be confident you can create a great marketer with the right amount of mentorship, guidance, and training. This is especially important if you're in a small company that can't afford a big-market superstar digital marketing manager who commands a minimum of $120,000 a year. You're going to be forced to think about hiring the way Major League Baseball teams think about farm teams. Index for potential, personality, and grittiness and be willing to invest the time and energy required to create a great marketer, and you'll be pleased with the outcome.

Another critical note on hiring is to stay within the general confines of your industry and your company size. I'm not encouraging uniformity or dependence on someone's previous skill set; it's merely that you can only expect so much flexibility from the average human being. I've seen far too many 10-person companies hire a hotshot marketing director from a Fortune 500 company who fails miserably in the first 60 days—because that person is an architect, not a doer. Their previous role involved three managers, a high-dollar agency, and a predictable pace. The new small-company environment requires someone to dive in and get his or her own hands dirty. These two worlds almost never mesh, so ignore how utterly amazing someone's resume is and how great their previous results appear.

"Industries" is also shorthand for business models. It's impossible to underestimate the difference between running marketing at an SaaS company versus a consumer packaged goods (CPG) company. The SaaS company is medieval in its focus on a sales funnel and revenue-repeatable processes and spending, whereas a CPG company is a brand-driven, channel-relationship optimization play of the highest order. These two models are so different that it'd be amazingly rare to find someone who excelled at both. Think of it as your 'marketing DNA'; marketing within a specific business model builds certain competencies that might not only be worthless in the other world; they might also actually harm the new effort.

Although I might seem overly insular about certain aspects of hiring, I'll reiterate that *potential* should be the basis for almost every decision. Don't expect someone with more than 5 to 7 years of marketing to completely unlearn one approach and excel at a new one. Be realistic and make smart decisions. Although hiring across industries can be risky, I've also seen it work out phenomenally well when the new staff brings never-before-seen tactics to the new marketing effort—for example, when someone comes into a traditional email-driven marketing group from a mobile-heavy industry in which short-message service (SMS) and in-app messaging are a regular part of the communications process. Your customers are probably way more ready than you are to meet them in these new communications destinations.

inally, let's talk about how the typical executive (CMO or ~~c~~ ɔuld approach the process of hiring directors and managers for their teams. At this level, it's less about raw potential and more about market approach and management style. Although you should always be dedicated to growing your people, the main selection criteria here should be who can drive the most meaningful change with the least amount of executive coaching and intervention. You need top-tier performers who thrive on pressure, can keep a team strong and motivated, and are deeply self-motivated.

A couple things I always look for include a wide personal network of peers (to drive downstream hiring and best-practices transfer); a predisposition to do and not just talk (resume and interview topics should be results-oriented and specific to their personal role in the success); and a strong sense of team-building (marketing is perpetually full of 20-something newcomers, and knowing how to hire and get the most from this generation is an art form itself).

And Finally, Your Technology Stack

If the right people are the ideal base to build your new behavioral-marketing approach, then technology is what will allow you to scale that effort. We've discussed and defined the ideas behind behavioral at length—and there's lots more coming up. Now, let's talk about the minimum technology pieces it takes to become a great behavioral marketer.

First, you need some decent competency—and a clear business driver—for the email channel. Email truly is the dream channel for behavioral marketing, given its ability to scale to millions of customers but address them via a single message. Although it is not always easy to split hairs that finely, email's automation and scale capabilities make it the perfect place to start.

There's a solution for almost any size company on the planet. I recently saw a number that calculated the number of email service providers (ESPs) at more than 350 in just the United States. There are likely dozens more internationally, so there's bound to be one for almost everyone who's in the market for one.

My advice on how to best choose an ESP normally requires answers to some pretty straightforward questions: How much is your budget, how big is your list, and how automated do you want to be? If you're just getting started and need something free that grows into ~$2,000 a year, there are some great choices in the market. Recognize you're likely going to share an IP address (and reputation scores as a result), but things should be cool until your list gets to six digits. If you're in hypergrowth mode and sell via email (such that deliverability is critically important) and want to begin the behavioral marketing journey with a couple of million customers, there are also many solutions under ~$75,000 a year. However, you need to be careful in this segment. Features and functionality start to become critically important, and you want to be very specific during your selection process. For the full-on enterprise play that requires integration with other back-end systems and needs to support both millions of records and expanded data structures, there are many players in the above $75,000 a year price range. A word of caution for this vendor segment: make sure which features are included versus those that are charged at additional fee.

You need a rock-solid email platform that can be the beginnings of your behavioral marketing machine. Don't choose a product that can't tie into your other business systems and don't buy so much cost per thousand (CPM)-based volume that you'll never use it all. Find a tool that matches your future-state automation desires and meets your price requirements today. And once you choose a tool, jump in with both feet. Integrate your key systems quickly and get down to work bringing behavioral marketing to life. Choosing the perfect email platform will mean nothing if you use it to only 10 percent of its potential.

The other required piece of technology to begin the behavioral marketing process is a centralized customer database. Many times, a good email platform can and will serve this function. It's even better if the platform's capabilities extend into the marketing automation space, allowing it to generate more rules-based automated campaigns on your behalf. In some organizations in which marketing and sales are heavily integrated, it's also common to see a full-blown CRM system. When pairing a strong CRM and a leading marketing automation system, make sure to carefully architect customer IDs and sources of reference data. The worst-case scenario is ending up with duplicate records that sales and marketing are working on separately. Trial this functionality deeply before releasing it widely across both departments, and make sure to dig deep during the selection process. A check box on a product slick is very different from seeing your test data smoothly synching between platforms.

The good news is that this is about all the must-have technology you need to get started with behavioral marketing. The most aggressive groups also have print-on-demand platforms to execute one-off direct-mail pieces; external agencies to build and maintain the absolute best creative, integrated call-center systems that populate all email campaigns sent to a specific customer the moment a rep picks up a call from them; and a powerful cross-channel reporting dashboard that sums it all up. But those aren't first-step requirements. You can build toward world-class by continuing to make incremental improvements in how you execute every single day.

If you're already running down the road of behavioral marketing, then your frame of reference should soon become channel orchestration. By outlining personal-level customer journey maps based on deep customer insights, you can begin to think about the relative strengths of each channel you have and how they can seamlessly collaborate. Supporting your ideal customer's buying process is a phenomenal place to start your next chapter of behavioral marketing prowess.

Part Two
Putting Behavioral Marketing Into Action

4 Pacing Yourself

Behavioral Marketing at the Speed of Business

I've been a digital marketer for more than 20 years, and I know how difficult it can be to move to new paradigms. I remember the first days of banner advertising, when we overpaid for cost-per-thousand impressions (CPMs) and tracked them in Excel spreadsheets. We had no idea if any of those clicks amounted to anything close to conversion, but we were out there trying. Eventually those tools would be powered by DoubleClick, which Google purchased, and AdWords as we know it today was born.

There's a similar movement taking place right now in the behavioral marketing space. Lots of brands are aggressively experimenting with this newish technology, and most show strong results. Being more relevant and personalized across your marketing programs is almost always a good thing—and drives more revenue virtually every time out.

Unlike the AdWords example, I don't believe a single company will consolidate the industry with a genius mergers and acquisitions (M&A) move. Instead, becoming a great behavioral marketer requires looking inward at your efforts and business, rather than standardizing a set of tasks on an external platform. We'll all be evaluating our marketing stack to make sure it gets us to our destination—but I'm pretty sure we're not all going to migrate our tech to a single company's service.

If you agree, you'll certainly want to make sure that your tech selections support an open integrated ecosystem.

And because we're all on our own journey to improve our own skills, technology, and results, we're all on a different path forward. A resource-constrained small business might have monetary hurdles that prevent them from getting beyond a free or supercheap solution to move into a bonafide behavioral marketing platform. If you're a huge multinational Fortune 100 company, you might not have tried behavioral marketing yet because your current marketers have been executing the same way for the last five years.

Whatever the reason, the best way to get on the path is to think about building out this capability at the speed of business. That is to say—you don't need to completely solve it this quarter or even this year. If you're really pushing hard, you should be outlining a one- to three-year vision for how to further integrate behavioral marketing into your mix. Your short-term plan should involve enhancing campaigns and audience selection methods, and you should be plotting system integrations and staffing upgrades for the long term.

Taking on Behavioral Marketing at Any Role

To illustrate the point, I'm going to break down the organizational structure we discussed in the last chapter and discuss how each role might begin to factor for behavioral marketing. Although it might seem like overkill to read about **every** role, depending on what yours is, it's critical to remember one important thing: anyone can undertake these tactics. Understanding how those both above and below you in the organizational structure are thinking about improving marketing's performance can be very insightful in plotting your future plans. So keep those minds open, and let's begin with the specialist role.

If you're the junior person in the group, you're typically going to have to manufacture your own opportunities to prove your skills and intelligence. Hopefully, your manager is helpful and is teaching you the real-life marketing skills while you transition from book knowledge to getting it done every day. Even—and maybe **especially**—if they're not, you should be looking for places to add value. That value often comes in the form of insights that others might overlook or not consider for as long as you might.

For example, you should be poring over every report of key performance indicators (KPIs) and looking deeply at the performance numbers behind the marketing efforts. Your undertrained eye may not spot everything, but think logically about cost versus reward. Look at top-line numbers—like how much your brand spends on paid media—and then look at program performance over the same time period. Are the larger investments paying dividends or are you wasting money? You can uncover these types of directional, data-driven trends by digging deep into the data—a task many marketers simply don't take the time to do.

Let me take a second and share a few tips for the new kid on the block. It's very much a question of personal style, but working most closely with your direct manager is usually the best way to consistently compel bottom-up change. You don't have to give her or him your best ideas to take as their own, but impressing your boss with your work ethic and thinking is normally your most effective path forward. Yes, there is the occasional case where the boss is a moron and you may be tempted to take your great idea to the director, but that rarely works out in your favor—particularly because your manager is probably insecure enough to take it as a personal slight regardless of how mind-blowingly great the idea may be. If you're in that crappy spot, start making the move to change companies (or divisions inside a really big company). Or decide to wait out the scenario. The important lesson here is choose your direct boss **VERY** carefully next time around.

So although the specialist must work hard to be seen and heard, the type of change behavioral marketing represents is absolutely the main job of every marketing manager. You are the primary doer, and you can unlock a ton of potential by thinking more deeply and working just a bit harder. And the great news is you don't need all kinds of permissions from your executives to get started. Actually, you might just work with your direct report to rethink some KPIs or look for performance improvements in content strategy.

Make no mistake: a strong orientation toward data and action is a great thing for your career. Unfortunately, many marketers have to change jobs to get promoted—particularly early in your career, when there's a natural stack-ranking going on among you and your peers. By overindexing for both the art and science of marketing discussed in the last chapter, you'll set yourself apart from others and put yourself on a much faster path to director—and beyond. If you can think critically like a VP (by understanding the VP role and motivation) and then extrapolate that into changes you can make, you'll move ahead quickly. Trust me—driving more revenue with the same resources is the magic trick that gets you promoted most often.

If you're a director, then bringing behavioral marketing to life will have some downstream skills requirements. You're not likely to have your hands in the day-to-day execution, so you'll need a team sharp enough to take your lead and run with it. As with almost every role, you can make some smaller moves independently (like beginning the customer journey mapping process we discuss later). But properly motivating your team to move toward ever more customer centricity should be your primary task.

In addition to properly motivating your team, the director should begin the selling-up process. Anyone in this role should be close enough to marketing execution to see the opportunity for upside and savvy enough to position it in terms your executives can understand and get behind. If anyone's in charge of building a pure business case to transform your marketing, it's the director. In general, I think about the director role as the chief change agent and improvement boss for that channel. You can't wait for your executives to request improvements, or you may have already lost the battle.

At the VP level, transforming your marketing to be more behavioral-driven is normally a question of channel orchestration and customer focus. Very few VPs I've ever met want to spend more money or do less marketing—unless there's a clear business case to reprioritize channel spending. By embracing the core tenets of behavioral marketing and assessing each channel's capability to deliver, the VP has the opportunity to perform like an air traffic controller. For example, you can divert funds from outdoor advertising to double-down on cart abandon email programs if need be.

And the opportunity to merchandise your team's success upward is a huge credibility opportunity with your SVP or CMO. They're looking at you to drive incremental revenue from marketing activities, and showing them hard data from newly launched campaigns that convert at 10 to 20 times over your standard batch-and-blast mailings signals a significant accomplishment. You might have to teach them a bit about the new behavioral capabilities and make sure they clearly understand they're part of an overall mix of truly effective marketing—mostly because you don't want them to think they can cut 90 percent of your budget and get the same revenue!

And finally, if you're a CMO and considering behavioral marketing as a discipline, remember that it's all about optimizing spend and keeping your marketing machine moving forward toward the future. I won't beat the dead horse regarding the average tenure of a new CMO remaining around 24 months, but, clearly, being more responsive to customer needs and leveraging data are huge top-level initiatives that CMOs are driving down into their organizations to increase revenue.

Great behavioral marketing done right uncovers untapped revenue that's close to closing but that you just can't count on yet. If you are an ecommerce seller, ensuring that your commerce team is crushing the cart, browse abandon campaigns can be the difference of thousands of dollars in revenue per month (and the bigger your average cart, the higher the return). You can bring to life the central tenets of measurement and data-driven decision making for both B2B and B2C longer-lead sellers with behavioral scoring and a perfectly designed content strategy that meets the customer at every step in the buyer's journey. This is not science fiction marketing from the future that requires a bench full of overpaid PhDs to execute. Have the forward-looking vision to challenge your teams to think more deeply about the customer, and be open to revising or even adding job requirements in the future that further the behavioral focus.

Although every role can bite off its own chunk of behavioral marketing, the true power comes when a couple of levels line up to prioritize it from an overall marketing perspective. Maybe it's just a director along with the email and database marketing managers who decide to move the approach forward. Or, ideally, it could be a top-down mantra, and all team members jump in, feet-first, and bring it to reality for their role every day.

At the Speed of Business

We close this chapter with some thoughts on how you can (and will be allowed to) spend money on behavioral marketing—both hard external dollars on technology and vendors, and human resource (HR) dollars on permanent headcount and contractors. No marketer should ever think they're going to get additional money to do anything they can't prove to be a winner first. That might sound ominous, but assuming you'll get nothing and having to sell every budget line item is more often the reality. So why not put yourself in that mode from the beginning?

This also means that getting a new marketing automation platform to execute all this might have to wait three months until the first quarter, when the financial results for holiday season are in the can. However, this doesn't mean you cannot—or should not—do anything until then.

Take your best shot at personalized communications with the tools you have now; show small but steady lift in testing among small groups. Be creative.

And yes—you're going to need an executive sponsor for most major technology upgrades and new headcount—unless you're the chief marketing officer and want to move some budget or job requirements around. Be keenly aware of your company's annual budgeting cycle and the requirements needed. And of course, someone needs to step up and be the face of the request process. Although the VP is normally the natural candidate for this, I've seen a hotshot director pull it off as well. Whoever leads the contingency will be the chief consensus builder among marketing as well as across the organization. Remember, it's almost always a fixed-sized pie and marketing competes for funding against sales, accounting, and customer support. Make sure you're buttoned-up and compelling in your argument, base it on revenue lift, and be prepared to defend it against all forms of other programs for budget allocation.

At the same time, I always counsel growing companies to be planning ahead aggressively. Even if you're not ready to buy this quarter, you might want to be investigating world-class SaaS tools as a director. Speak to your peers at other companies or search out analyst content on the topic. Having your desired solution laid out in broad strokes is a very smart plan—especially if you're venture-backed and there's a round of funding on the horizon. Venture firms dole out money based on the idea that they can drive geometric progression in terms of revenue, and behavioral marketing can be a great tactic to gain quick wins.

Understand the market and company dynamics continually swirling around you, and be fully prepared to strike when the opportunity presents itself. Cultivate your go-to advocates in marketing; spend time talking to sales about increasing efficiencies between your groups to close more deals; and be ready to accept the role of change agent. Almost every marketing group in the developed world is going to have to figure out how to be more personalized and focused on customer behaviors. Go invent the future.

5 Bringing Behavioral Marketing to Life in the Real World

Now that we've assessed where you stand in terms of behavioral marketing, and charted the people and process course for moving forward, let's dive into the **how**. The next six chapters look carefully at what behavioral marketing means to almost every marketing channel and activity. But scoping the pace and method for taking on a newer way to think about marketing takes time and some deeper consideration.

Conversely, you should not overanalyze enhancements to your marketing approach, because all this will do is make them much more difficult to achieve. Incremental change driven by a relentless pursuit of improvements will set a comfortable pace for most marketers.

The "Next Six" Methodology

One of the most common questions I get from our customers is how to reframe their marketing to be more behavioral-driven, while continuing to execute the tasks and campaigns they're currently working on. It almost always comes down to a question of priorities and how hard you want to work. No marketer I know should expect a reprieve of their daily duties so they can think deeply about being more behavioral. You must accept upfront that you're going to have to change the tires on a moving car.

The best way to make this change part of your program over time is to improve in smaller chunks, typically in groups of three and over a specified period of time (like a quarter). In all the years I've worked as a marketer, making incremental improvements along the way has been achievable. Making audience selection smarter, turning on a simple scoring model, or getting my IT partners to install the JavaScript tracking tool on the website are all examples of one-off projects I could manage easily alongside my regular work.

The brilliance of this simpler view of change is that you only have to architect changes in groups of three to support a larger change initiative. And if you tackle three of these per quarter, you can certainly remake your marketing approach in the course of 12 to 18 months.

I call this the "Next Six" method because you should always be in execution mode on three, and on planning mode on the next three—at an absolute minimum. If you're really good, and you've been successful with your first six, you might even think in increments of 12 and be focused on some bigger, hairier issues that involve other internal groups. For example, you may be looking forward to big enterprise initiatives like integrating your marketing automation platform with your customer-relationship manager (CRM) or combining your marketing automation platform with your Content Management System (CMS) so you can tailor websites at the individual level based on behavior.

Take the time to fully articulate your future state at 12, 18, and 24 months. Be very specific about what capabilities you'd like to have, and then back into the changes required to get there. Recognize that some change will require only you, but bigger transformations may well impact others in your organization—specifically IT, customer support, sales, and other key groups. If it sounds like you just spooled up an entire change management practice for marketing, it's because **you did**. Embrace it, and begin the process.

One of the most common protests I hear from marketers is they don't have the time to do things differently—and, unfortunately, it's one I am more likely to hear from a more experienced marketer. There's a set-in-my-ways dynamic in the marketing function—especially when management isn't forcing the change down the reporting structure.

So yes—you may very well have to work a few extra hours a week to get this going. But the truth is that most of us could be more efficient with our daily tasks and find the time. Let's say, for the sake of argument, that you're 100 percent deployed for your 40-hour workweek. Setting aside two days a week (Tuesday and Thursday, to keep it easy) to spend an extra 45 minutes at the end of your day scoping and planning this behavioral future is an investment that will pay off.

A Real-Life Example

It's easy to talk about in theory, so let's dive right into a real-world blueprint, with the example of a small-scale retailer who has both an online presence and physical stores. Let's say we're in a heavily contested category like nutrition, and that our email list has 50,000 opted-in recipients and we have 12 corporate-owned stores primarily in the Northeast and Mid-Atlantic states. Our marketing has been pretty routine to date, and our sales are relatively steady at 50/50 online to in-store. How would we chart the future course for such a business?

The first question I'd seek to answer with the executive leadership is about the sales ratio between online and in-store. Specifically, do we want to continue to keep that ratio well balanced, or do we want to expand our product offerings online and attempt to grow sales on that side of the business? What's our average sale value for each channel, and could we improve those numbers in one or both channels to help drive a different prioritization?

Second, I'd want to build out personas and characterize my customers' buying habits. Is the fact that we're in a competitive segment forcing us into discounting or can we maintain decent margins based on a solid marketing methodology combined with a differentiated product set? How aggressive have we been historically? Is there room for significant offer testing and maybe even a loyalty program? And do our online and retail personas differ significantly, or does the audience look and feel much the same across all channels?

Once you answer these top-line questions, we can move into program enhancement mode. Keep in mind that answering these first questions shouldn't take you 60 days and require absolute agreement from every stakeholder in your company. You can nail down directional answers early on, and be prepared to morph your future state as you go. Show me someone with an inflexible 18-month plan, and I'll show you someone who clearly doesn't have a solid grasp on how a business functions.

The first place to look for enhancements is in the digital marketing tier, specifically within the content you're currently delivering. Have you done some high-level A/B testing of subject lines to know what key phrases drive opens, clicks, and conversions with your email? You don't need to tackle full-on multivariate testing of every content block in your message, just understand if your audience responds better to product- or offer-oriented subject lines. What happens when you turn on limited-time offers like buy-one-get-one (BOGO) free or free shipping?

After email subject-line enhancements, begin tracking and segmenting your audience based on behaviors. Initially, this will require you to work with IT to install the JavaScript tracking code I reference throughout this book (including the definitions section in Chapter 1). This one-time effort opens up a critical customer-level view of behaviors that should flow directly into your marketing automation platform and become elements you can query on immediately.

Along with content enhancements, you want to be thinking about list growth as an ongoing effort. Most retailers I know fully expect to be losing somewhere around 20 percent of their list to attrition of all forms on an annual basis. Keeping your list strong and clean isn't something that happens without a serious plan. As we'll discuss shortly, in-store registration is a huge source of name acquisition, but having a strong digital-side approach is important as well. One of the best ways to drive this behavior is to build out a strong content strategy based on knowledgeable recommendations and feed it with an ultratargeted paid media campaign on very specific search terms.

This is also a great time to consider a simple scoring model to help you segment your audience based on activity. Assign point values to email opens, buy now clicks, website page visits, and any other number of user-generated actions. Creating an objective score for each one of your users will allow you to then identify which of your best customers should receive different content or better offers. Or you might segment out your least active customers for your best reactivation offers in order to drive "one more transaction this quarter."

An ideal way to round out digital enhancements is to build and launch three to four key behavior-driven automated programs. The first would definitely be cart abandon, and I'd spend some serious thought time on the pace and content of each of at least three messages. The first should be within 30 minutes of abandon, the second should come the next day and feature an offer, and the final should happen two days later and make your absolute best case for the purchase.

The second automated program would be a browse abandon campaign, which I'd pilot on my most profitable line of products. Once a named user visits one or more specific product pages in that category, the program should automatically trigger a message featuring the best sellers in the category, and potentially include an offer. By playing back content we know the person is interested in, we very subtly reinforce that we're paying attention, thereby driving the personalization quotient through the roof. Many of these browse abandon campaigns convert at 150–200 percent of standard bulk messaging, and put us squarely on the path toward proving the monetary value of behavioral marketing.

The last automated program I'd build would be a comprehensive three to four touch welcome campaign designed for new registrants to my list. It would begin with a simple thank you message, move on to content about both my online and retail stores, and close with an offer designed to drive the first purchase event. The beauty of a well-orchestrated welcome process is that it creates an instant deeper bond with a recipient as compared to just ignoring the signup event. Keep it personal, light, and informative and you'll build a quick rapport with your newest customers, which often leads to more profitability down the road.

The retail side could begin with something typically beyond the scope of marketing yet critical to the success of the business. Assess the skill level and training methods currently in place for employees. Is your company hiring for, and maintaining, a deeper level of nutritional knowledge, or are they simply filling the slots with hourly workers? What kind of employee communications program could you build that would deliver product and lifestyle information to the 50 to 60 employees who help your customers in person every day across your store network? In almost every case, a more highly trained and insightful store rep means more sales.

Second, I'd make sure my store sales information was as readily available as my ecommerce sales information. Most often, this means pushing some level of customer information down into a point-of-sale (POS) system that tracks retail purchases at the individual level. This should also be a secondary point of email opt-in, and, in a perfect world, there should be a single view of the customer across both ecommerce and retail. I know one major U.S.-based retailer who now drives more than 60,000 new email opt-ins per month since they enhanced their POS system and in-store processes to support that effort.

Once you've solidified this single customer view, you can bring the core elements of a loyalty program to market pretty easily. You can create levels of your program based on spending, and then begin managing each segment's communications differently. Given the operation's relatively small size, I'd likely skip the physical card and monthly statement aspects of a traditional loyalty program and go for a POS enhancement that would print the points balance on every receipt—and a function so any store rep could pull up a specific user's balance. Your POS system should also seamlessly manage any coupon or promotional code redemption.

Beyond the technology side of running a loyalty program, you must train your store reps on the program's details. There's no worse customer experience than showing up at retail with a question about a promotion or loyalty program, and the staff knows nothing of the program details.

Finally, I'd be looking to drive in-store sales via digital programs for the retail side. Since there are only 12 physical locations, this won't work for your entire audience, but I'd segment out and begin marketing slightly differently to everyone within a 10-mile radius of your stores. I might experiment with in-store events (think manufacturer rep days or evening guest speakers) as a way to extend your buying experience for online-only customers to visit your physical stores. You could also seek to build a community of your customers around certain affinities. Maybe your location is the meeting place for a local cycling group, or you host weekly weight management meetings—anything that will bring your customers together around your physical locations.

You can chart these goals in whatever format makes sense for you and your business, but you'll want to include the impacts on other groups along the way. You may opt for a classic timeline view you can easily tape to your wall to track high-level progress, or go full depth and build out business requirements and work streams for every impacted group. Much of your documentation approach should be based on how much support your colleagues need to drive change.

The changes we have discussed here could easily take a marketer 8 to 12 months to bring to fruition while managing the rest of their work. It's always exciting to think about the end state, but remember how much effort and planning it takes to add this type of change to your everyday queue of work.

Reasons We Fail

Although all this change sounds pretty straightforward when reading about it, it's hard work in reality. I constantly speak to marketers who have tried to make progress on one or two initiatives, but can't get things going. Worse yet, they get halfway there and momentum simply stalls out. To that end, the next section discusses four common scenarios and how I've seen marketers navigate past them to success.

1. **No executive support:** Among the most common issues I hear from directors and managers is that their executives aren't explicitly asking for this kind and level of effort—and, therefore, aren't necessarily in favor of them spending lots of time on it. Sometimes you have to operate beyond the scope of your more classically trained executive team. There are plenty of market conditions to indicate that behaviors are the new measurement equivalent of transactions in terms of understanding customers' experiences.

Sure, your VP may not be asking you for KPIs like percentage of complete data records, but that doesn't mean you shouldn't take that to them. Chapter 16 discusses the importance of using behavioral marketing methods to set yourself apart from other marketers—and to drive promotion and new job opportunities outside your current company. This is the time to go beyond what's expected to what's possible, and to capitalize on the upside you create.

2. **No internal support:** For every marketer who tells me their boss doesn't get it, there are 20 that have a completely legitimate complaint against their peers inside the organization—often beginning in IT, and crossing almost every discipline. It's not common to find serious change agents looking to radically improve marketing capabilities across groups like sales and finance. Human nature is to not upset the proverbial apple cart—to be content with minor enhancements that are easy to roll out.

   This is where I recommend marketers aggressively build their network across the company well before they request major changes in thinking. Spend a couple of months building close relationships and giving as much as you can to create good will. Be an evangelist for the marketing function, offer your help in customer-facing programs—in short, do everything you can to help your colleagues.

   Although this is true in almost any company, it becomes all the more important as your organization becomes larger. I've personally worked in eight-person startups where I was the complete marketing function, and I've been a marketing thought leader at two Fortune 50 companies—UPS and IBM—that each have somewhere north of 400,000 employees each. As the company gets larger, so do the complexities, and the only true way to combat this phenomenon is to self-define as a change agent, and aggressively seek out others like you across the organization.

And let's be honest—some days, the best strategy in a big company is to break your big third-quarter goal down into two to three smaller component pieces and reset for next year. You're not going to win every single battle, and sometimes being pragmatic is the best move to keep your allies strong and your objectives within reach on the horizon.

3. **Not enough time:** This is almost always the first objection of the first attempt to remake your marketing effort around behavioral marketing. Marketers come to an event or a strategy session and leave supercharged and ready to get behavioral. They might even get back to the office and start some A/B subject line testing, but they don't make meaningful progress over the next 6 to 12 months.

   This is the normal state of affairs, but it's my personal goal in business to make sure fewer marketers fall into this trap. If you can't get this done during the course of your regular job, then I'd contend you simply need to work harder. Again, easy to say but harder to do. I've seen literally dozens of cases in which a marketing manager takes greater charge of the role and responsibilities and ends up being a director more quickly or getting an increase in salary next time reviews come around.

   The net here is whether you want to stand out or slot into a marketing role. It's very clear that the luxury of being an order taker is going to evaporate within the next three to four years. Right now, there's a 22-year-old graduating from a great school that's learned how to measure marketing programs and doesn't know any other way. Don't be the deer-in-the-headlights who gets run down by this class of up-and-coming new-school marketers.

4. **Underwhelming results:** Every once in a while, I'll run across someone who has tackled the hard work but whose results just don't pan out as strongly as expected. Maybe their cart abandon campaign only converts 10 percent of recipients instead of a category-leading

30 percent. And maybe the difficult task of executing data strategy hasn't paid off in revenue lift as expected.

This requires us to be brutally honest with ourselves. Did we *really* give it 110 percent, or did we only make first-order changes to a broken process that now is only 10 percent more efficient? Like everything in life, not every behavioral marketing move is going to work out perfectly. The difference between being successful in this new world is whether you continue to execute the plan.

One pro tip: if you're fortunate enough to be self-starting these initiatives and don't have top-down pressure, save your sharing moments until *after* you've proven revenue or customer satisfaction lift. No one says you have to go all the way out on the ledge before execution, and tip your hand on strategy and results. Oftentimes, it's much more compelling to report the final results of your test in successful terms—even if it takes a few cycles to get the tactics correct.

Overall, marketers should begin the first steps of reorienting around behavioral-marketing principles with a reality check. Understanding the advantages and disadvantages going into the process will help improve your end results. And perhaps the fact that you've built an amazing relationship with your CIO will pay epic dividends when it comes time to integrate CRM data back into your marketing automation system.

You're going to have to chart a course that's unique to your industry and business, but remember that bad things rarely happen when we're relentlessly moving forward. Be thoughtful and realistic, but don't hold back—more often than not, history rewards the brave, even in corporate marketing.

6 Upping Your Content Game

Educating Customers Throughout the Entire Cycle

I f there's one topic that I speak with marketers about most often other than responsive design, it's the rise of content strategy as a marketing tactic. There are lots of blogs and books on this singular topic alone, but I want to cover this subject here as a now-required tactic among the most behavioral-oriented marketers. Content serves all kinds of critical roles within our traditional marketing effort, and to think it doesn't apply even more so to digital is downright false.

Depending on whose data you believe, customers make between 50 percent and 70 percent of their buying decision before ever interacting with a brand. (The Corporate Executive Board put this number at 57 percent as long ago as 2012, so one can only imagine how that number has grown since then.) This means that web-based research, social media recommendations, product reviews, and dozens of other content touch points all inform an opinion about our product or services before a prospect ever even talks to us. This also means we're likely to be asked very end-game questions when the call or email actually shows up. Getting customer requests like best price, custom configurations, or determining whether the item is in stock are the symptoms of failing to focus more effectively on content earlier in the buyer's journey.

I think back to the last new vehicle I bought. In general, I almost always buy directly from manufacturers' certified pre-owned programs; but in 1999, as I saw the initial images of the first-year redesigned Ford F-350 Crew Cab Dually, I was hooked. I absolutely had to have that vehicle. Being the research geek I am, I set out to understand every possible configuration, option, color, and price. I scoured Ford.com, Edmunds, truck magazines, Kelley Blue Book, and lots of other websites.

The really interesting dynamic occurred when I showed up to preorder the truck at one of the highest volume Ford dealers in the nation: I knew more about the truck than anyone at the dealership. We sat down to write the order, and I was giving the sales rep the codes for each option and package. And, of course, I knew the MSRP, invoice cost, and actual dealer cost numbers—so we had a nice data-driven negotiation about how little over actual cost I was going to pay. Remember, it was a guaranteed sale for the dealer, and he'd never have to spend a dime in marketing or incentives on the truck—so I wanted the best price possible.

The interesting outcome was that I ended up using a high-touch, high-dollar channel essentially as pure fulfillment. If I could have clicked the same buttons the sales rep did, I could have given Ford $35,000 without speaking to virtually anyone. And if this was true in 1999, imagine how much more access our prospects and customers have to data about us now. And imagine what immense pressure brands like Amazon place on retailers like Best Buy and Target. "Show-rooming," that is, checking competitor prices on a smartphone while standing in an aisle where they could simply purchase the item on the spot—is now an accepted part of many consumer's buying process. As a result, these retailers have been forced to price match in order to capture the revenue—even if they have to give away 10–12 percent of margin to get it.

Although creating great content that forces a buyer to move through a specific channel can be very tricky, there are many examples in which the right content at the right moment is enough to tip the conversion scales. Or at a minimum, it maintains a conversation over time while the buyer is considering all the options including price.

Let's consider how you could think about mapping content to four unique buying scenarios. Although certain markets expect specific types of content (for instance, complex technical sales almost always feature product feature sheets), one of the most progressive tactics I've seen in the last 12 to 18 months is brands creating all new types of content. We cover some examples throughout this chapter, but it's seizing the opportunity to do something different from your direct competitor that is critical to impressing your prospect or customer.

Let's look at these four specific customer interaction points, and how you can support each one with great content strategy:

1. Acquisition.
2. Prospect nurturing.
3. Retention/loyalty.
4. Postpurchase.

Acquisition is potentially the most critical time to ensure you've articulated—and are effectively delivering—a comprehensive content strategy. This is especially true in B2B marketing, where it's now a required tactic. If you don't have a proactive outreach strategy (often an elegant combination of social, search, and paid media) supported by deep thought leadership content that educates the marketplace, then you're simply missing the mark. Your job as a marketer is to proactively seek ideal customers for your company, and to be razor-sharp at converting them into paying customers.

This is how many small startups are able to effectively mount a challenge to large-market incumbents. Think about small-business services companies like Square, which singlehandedly democratized the process of accepting credit cards for small businesses and single-person companies. Or Buffer, which has demystified social media management to the point that a single person can manage multiple networks on behalf of multiple brands simultaneously. Both companies have built their brand around removing the friction from a previously miserable customer experience, and, as a result, enjoy awareness among millions of growing businesses each year based on a brilliant combination of business value and timely, insightful content that advances the skill level of their customers.

Beyond B2B, there are both big and small B2C brands who have figured out that lifestyle-driven content does a great job on creating a conversation with new prospective users, and that a selling opportunity might be months or years away but keeping that relationship warm is critical. You see very targeted examples of this with huge brands like Red Bull. I use them as a fully scaled example because they've taken lifestyle marketing to another level in the last two to three years. Beyond Formula One sponsorship (including epic Infiniti racing events all over the world), they've even taken the extraordinary step of creating a print magazine called *The Bulletin* that's 100 percent made up of lifestyle content. Add that to extreme sports tie-ins they manage with athletes from every sport (even space jumping with Austrian skydiver, daredevil, and BASE jumper Felix Baumgartner), and it's clear the Red Bull brand desires a long-term, lifestyle-driven conversation with new and existing customers designed to keep their energy drink products and brand top-of-mind with a very desirable demographic.

Prospect Nurturing

Again, this is a bread-and-butter strategy for selling to businesses in a B2B scenario. I'll use my role with Silverpop as an example here. My job as an evangelist is two-pronged: the first part involves counseling and mentoring digital marketers in-person, and helping them tackle their most difficult issues. On that front, I see approximately 100 customers annually. The other half of my role is more scale-oriented. Beyond one-to-one thought leadership, I have the task of writing three to four blog posts each quarter, doing about 50 speaking engagements a year, and developing various whitepapers, tip sheets, and authored articles each year. It's a bit like a professor's gig in the sense that it's "publish or die."

We've proven pretty effective at scaling this across our entire organization. There were less than 10 blog contributors when I joined in 2011. That number exceeds 25 today, and we put out 300 to 400 posts annually with all kinds of perspectives. We also deliver more than 20 whitepapers each year, which average 10 to 12 pages and represent a significantly deep dive on a specific topic.

So why do so many people across our organization take the two to three hours required to write an insightful blog post, that often? For the simple reason that all that content powers the conversation between Silverpop and our customers—both existing and prospective. Our deep library on all topics related to digital marketing allows our sales team to share strategy in support of specific product-oriented conversations. If someone wants to understand how behavioral marketing fits with a loyalty program, there are no fewer than four or five blog posts on that topic from the prior year.

We also undertake primary research to support our customers' and prospects' need to understand how to benchmark their existing pro-grams. Whether that's our annual *Email Benchmark Report* or the recent global research on Best Friend Brands (see Chapter 15), these are key content items that serve the absolutely critical role of educating our customers in exchange for them sharing more specific details about their marketing needs.

This type of multimonth or multiyear orchestration is a hallmark of almost every successful B2B brand, and, to put an execution-level fine point on it, I'll refer back to the previous chapter's discussion about scoring user behaviors. When broken down to their smallest component parts, you can and should score each piece of content—blog post, whitepaper, tip sheet, and so forth—separately. When you combine and map these scores over time, they provide an excellent view of who's most interested in your solution. There are very few tactics better at guiding a high-velocity sales team in how to deploy their resources against an always-shifting pipeline of prospects.

Although I've focused deeply on our own B2B thinking around lead nurturing, I know many consumer-facing brands who apply many of the same tactics to derive an "engagement" score as opposed to a "propensity-to-buy" score. By understanding which customers are regularly opening their emails, repeatedly viewing high-value SKUs, and interacting with lifestyle-oriented content, they're able to build highly active segments and equally inactive segments.

Often, it's critical to monitor the inactive customers in B2C because high-volume senders seek to keep their email reputation clean at the Internet Service Provider (ISP) level. Most progressive retailers have either a manual or automated version of list cleanup that concentrates their efforts on those who have opened or clicked in the last 9 to 12 months. To ignore inactive users and continue to blast away almost always leads to deliverability pain. This is why understanding who *isn't* consuming your content can be just as important as knowing who is. For an even deeper dive on dealing with inactive users—or disinterested recipients as I call them—see Chapter 12.

Retention/Loyalty

Although the specific types of content may not change radically across each of these disciplines (white papers, blog posts, etc.), the focus of each must represent the specific phase the customer is in. When thinking through customer retention and loyalty, the best marketers I know are seeking to deepen both the product and the emotional connection between the user and the solution they're using. Beyond features and efficiency, this is the time to inspire your customers to be better at their jobs—to be promoted more often or to enjoy their own success more deeply.

For example, think about all the small business-related content that's created by accounting brands as large as Intuit or as niche as my friends Steve Bristol and Allan Branch's business, LessAccounting. Both brands understand that accounting is a relatively unwelcome task for every small business owner and they seek to reduce the stress via better software. The difference in the big-company version of the offering (QuickBooks) is a software-level feature race, but the niche version of the offering (LessAccounting) is more focused on "making accounting suck less." Both solve the business problem, but I'll give you two guesses which brand engenders more passion and dedication. Yep it's the nimble, irreverent brand that empathizes with its user base and seeks to alleviate the annoyance of the task.

This is also a perfect time to reaffirm your customers' choice of your product or service, and to begin a dialogue about them contributing content that will further turbocharge your marketing efforts. Reaching out to request community participation or app reviews, or asking satisfied customers to take reference calls from prospects in their industry are all great ways to leverage your satisfied customers into another positive content moment.

If you're really hitting on all cylinders, you'll want a very proactive case study function that builds a library of content you can share with both customers and other key audiences like the press and analyst firms. You should be prepared to produce and author the content yourself to ensure it works best for your objectives. In addition, most customers simply will not have time to dedicate to a noncore activity like this. If you're a prospective buyer and can read a case study of a satisfied customer in a similar industry, you'll be able to complete much of the presales work very quickly.

It's also important to engage your existing audience in advocate-level interactions across social media. Make it easy for them to tweet quotes from whitepapers with embedded social sharing links. This "social proof" is a critical aspect in almost every buyer's decision-making process. One of the fundamental reasons we attend technology conferences is to understand what and how our industry is thinking about a specific issue. If you can approximate that same peer dynamic via social media, you'll be operating at a very high level.

Postpurchase Content

Finally, let's focus on an ultraspecific version of targeted content that has come to market in the last 12 to 18 months, and it's almost exclusively a consumer-facing strategy. I first saw this tactic employed by one of our customers in an attempt to solve a very specific business problem that's a symptom of being a mainly online retailer of high-end sporting goods.

The company had a few retail outlets, and they clearly understood that many of their products depended on expertise delivered by a highly trained, experienced in-store rep. When it came to fitting ski boots appropriately, that in-person experience conveyed all the important details like how the boot should and shouldn't feel, correct fit, and suggested binding settings. Because the retailer was very good at web-based commerce in general, they found themselves selling an increasing number of these rather expensive ski boots via e-commerce.

But what started as a great thing for revenue turned into a returns issue over time. People were buying $300 to $400 ski boots, trying them on in their living rooms, and thinking they were the worst-fitting thing they'd ever placed on their feet. If you've ever been skiing, you know how utterly uncomfortable ski boots are right until the moment you point your skis down the hill. Right then, all the engineering is obvious and a great midmarket boot can make a *huge* difference in how much you enjoy a day of skiing.

To mitigate this returns issue, the retailer developed an ultraspecific two-touch postpurchase email campaign with a fully automated program based on a specific set of SKUs. The audience was anyone who had bought a pair of boots. Figure 6.1 shows what the first message looks like.

This simple recognition of a purchase, along with links to a fitting guide and more onsite content, went a very long way in reinforcing a high-dollar purchase in the buyer's fragile postpurchase, prereturn moment. Returns slowed down almost immediately, and the brand took advantage of the moment brilliantly.

Once they were confident they'd addressed the buyer's concerns with a well-executed multitouch campaign, they decided to test a cross-sell offer that looked like the one shown in Figure 6.2.

Hey there! So we heard you just got yourself some new ski boots - awesome! We wanted to be sure you have all the info you need to make you new boots fit perfectly. Click above or below to read the guide on how to try your boots on the right way. Stay tuned for more evo information (evormation?).

Click Here to Read More

Figure 6.1 First Message of an Ultraspecific Two-Touch Postpurchase Email Campaign

Don't forget socks with your next order! Now that you have some great, new, perfectly-fitting, ski boots it's time to finish it off with some comfy socks. Just remember, happy feet=happy snow days.

Click Here to Shop!

Figure 6.2 An Example of a Cross-Sell Offer to the Multitouch Campaign

And guess what? These postpurchase campaigns were among the most interactive emails they'd sent in months. Open rates were above 58 percent and the click-to-open rate was 45 percent—both incredibly strong numbers for a high-volume ecommerce retailer. The key here was clearly understanding a buyer's postpurchase mentality, and developing an effective multitouch campaign to reinforce that critical moment. Beyond supporting that single purchase, you can imagine the long-term customer satisfaction of buyers who are confident their favorite brand is personally vested in their happiness.

So Whose Job Is It?

Although it sounds easy on paper, great content strategy often requires many organizations—both brand new startups and fully established companies—to rethink roles. Your average sales pro probably isn't going to comprehend the subtlety required to architect this conversation, but on the other side of the spectrum, your 23-year-old social media manager isn't going to know your product and market cold. The key is to hire and train at least one marketing employee specifically to focus on content. Some days this means they'll create the content (think managing your company's Twitter presence); other days they'll lead others in the organization to create meaningful content in their areas of expertise.

So why isn't content just another marketing function we can assign to whoever's least busy? Because nowadays, this is how we first meet our customers. If you run a small shop in any city, would you scream at every person who walked through the door to buy something now? Managing a more subtle conversation that begins with you adding value, and one that supports the buyer's journey, has quickly become the norm. You're going to need to architect every step in that process—from a great welcome message to a free or low-cost trial designed to prove your value without enterprise-level investment, all the way through great postpurchase support. Leaving this to chance is a great way to find yourself struggling to stay in business 12 to 18 months from now.

Conclusion

The key takeaway when thinking about content is that **this** is your new form of customer acquisition. The best news is that it's nowhere near as expensive as the acquisition channels of the past—specifically TV advertising or an enterprise sales force. The worst news is that it's a new competency that you'd better solve for quickly before a smaller, faster competitor figures it out. Beyond the pure acquisition aspects, great content builds and supports highly personalized relationships that lead to more revenue per customer and higher buyer satisfaction over time.

Great content strategy isn't rocket science, but neither is it easy for just any company to execute. Developing your competency in this area of marketing will pay big dividends in the next 18 to 24 months as almost every buyer's expectation is raised beyond just a simple trans-action. The personal and informational relationship you build with your buyers will determine how quickly and how often they choose your product or service.

Don't miss this opportunity because it requires you to think slightly differently. Think of it as an all-new moment in the marketing spectrum where you might be able to grab some market share from a larger competitor—or at least improve the quality of your current relationships.

7 Customer Journey Mapping

Putting Yourself in the Customer's Shoes

When a company truly embraces behavioral marketing, the most fundamental shift is to reorient the entire effort around the customer. This might seem obvious, but walking that proverbial walk can be tough work for even the most progressive marketers.

The litmus test is no longer which product the business wants to push this quarter. The most popular—or highest margin—product isn't featured in every email in a given week or month. The marketer's job is to optimize the customer's buying journey, in whatever form that takes. Some days it'll be inspiring a prospect to become a first-time customer; other days it'll be perfecting the repeat buying behavior among your best customers that drives long-term, meaningful revenue growth.

The Current State of Customer Journey Mapping

Although there are some very advanced (and developing) concepts and tactics around customer journey mapping, I'm going to discuss it from the position of the typical digital marketer whose primary job is designing and delivering customer-facing campaigns. I make that distinction because there are increasingly important disciplines such as customer experience management that are still growing into a function that's common across industries and are housed within marketing departments.

Many of today's brands that are defining the best practices rise from industries such as financial services, consumer product goods, and automotive. And the reality is the function is still a bit like the total quality management of the 1980s and 1990s. Its function is concentrated in a small group that has to work in a matrixed environment across marketing, operations, finance, and so on. My take is that this keeps the function seminiche, and we'll continue to see innovation come from Fortune 100 brands and high-dollar agencies.

Let's take a much more practical look at how to think about factoring our own marketing efforts for customer journey mapping.

Starting with the Big Three

Although you could go crazy mapping dozens of customer journeys (or become obsessed with mapping a single, massive path to advocacy), let's focus on some more component pieces that turn out to be most actionable and meaningful to your revenue growth. We focus first on the pure acquisition journey, followed by the path to first purchase, and finally the path to repeat purchase (from the second buy through to implicit loyalty). As a means to illustrate this, I'm going to use a B2B software company as an example in each section.

Acquisition

Beyond the natural motivation marketers have to grow their lists, we need to clearly map out the first step in the journey with our prospects. First, we need to understand the existing match between our company's unique selling proposition and our prospect's needs and wants. Remember, if you have a fundamental disconnect at that level, no amount of brilliant marketing is going to save the day.

It's also critical to understand how to optimize your top-of-the-funnel resources to make sure you're spending time and money most effectively to create great prospects that convert to repeat customers. Relentlessly tracking conversion rates by unique lead source will highlight when we produce great content or buy the absolutely optimal paid media. Over time, this data should be used to guide content strategy, inform which events you invest in, and determine what (if any) paid media channels are reliable sources of paying customers for your business.

When mapping out the acquisition journey, make sure to factor for both demographic (gender, location, or level of spending) and behavioral (site visits or email opens) details along with lead source data. You should be seeking to build a persona-level profile of an ideal prospect. Make sure to build your data schema to factor for key elements such as gender, lifetime spending, geographic location, and other individual attributes you can use later to segment the audience. If in doubt about capturing a data point, ask yourself if you'd ever use that information to drive dynamic content in an email. If the answer is yes, undertake the effort to capture and save it.

For example, I have at least two customers who are actively tracking anonymous users in their marketing automation platform in order to understand which specific banner or keyword led them to an initial site visit. This data is also easy to track with web analytics tools like Google Analytics, but most often that places the data in an unfortunate silo. If click source is integrated at the record level within the marketing automation platform, we can then extend backward from all our known conversion events to determine which advertising sources (or keywords) are most predictably creating great customers. This data directly informs future ad spending, and the optimized circle is complete.

One of the questions I get often relates to how many data points to capture; but the real motivation of the question is return on investment (ROI). The real question should be: "How much time and effort should I spend on my data-collection strategy and implementing that can go into my campaign execution?" The answer is about 125 percent more than you think you should. Clearly not every two-person marketing department is going to have a 500-element customer record for 90 percent of their database, but most marketers could easily do more than they are doing today. And this increased customer understanding—at *any* point in the customer journey—is your best chance of driving deeper relevance and, therefore, more revenue.

From an acquisition perspective, it's not difficult to map out a prospect's first two or three likely journeys through your site. You should clearly articulate how you and the visitor both get your needs met, and how much insight you end up with at the conclusion of the initial visit. If it's a one-way street with you providing important information but not improving your customer understanding, that's a failure on your part that will cost you real dollars in uncaptured revenue. If you're asking for all the information without providing real value, you're in an even worse spot—and should probably seriously rethink your strategy.

Bottom line: the acquisition process is a value exchange. You provide insight, market data, and optimization strategies while your prospect provides behavioral and demographic data about themselves that gives you the necessary information to build great models. If it sounds like you have the hard job, then you're exactly right. If everyone was a great marketer or seller, or if crafting great content and campaigns were simple, there'd be no reward in the form of increased sales. You're in search of one elusive thing: a process that produces first-time buyers in a repeatable model. Understand and solve for that, and acquisition marketing will be a professional strength forever.

So for acquisition, our hypothetical B2B software company should be thinking very critically about where they spend their paid media dollars and tracking the interactions at the individual level in each location. By understanding the source of their most profitable leads over time (which requires solid lead source analysis) this can clearly inform where next year's dollars are going to be spent.

Also, understanding what types of message work best in the advertising is critical. Does your audience click and convert from deep product information or top-level market research content? Make sure there's enough diversity in your advertising content to be able to track the difference.

Path to First Purchase

This is a journey many marketers don't view as their primary job. Most marketers I know are happy enough to drive a certain quantity of leads to their sales force or to their ecommerce store. I'd argue this could be the source of the most improvement (and revenue growth) for any marketer. Let's look at two key reasons.

First, there's simply more responsibility and budget flowing to marketing departments as we become more measureable and able to succeed at a scale a sales force couldn't replicate. For example, even the biggest B2B sellers have moved to an aggressive presales process that has two critical outcomes: (1) it delivers an insanely qualified and quantified prospect to a sales resource; and (2) if the buyer's presales informational needs are straightforward, the sale actually closes without human intervention via a well-oiled marketing program. (This is a classic objective of great SaaS marketing in which your goal is often to qualify, sell, and onboard as efficiently as possible so your direct-sales resources are reserved for 10 huge-dollar deals as opposed to 1,000 small-dollar deals.) Sure, this means thinking more about self-service tools so these high-velocity customers don't have to revert to an old-style account support role, but imagine if stepping up your marketing game translated directly into an 8–10 percent lift in revenue.

Second, you absolutely cannot underestimate the importance of the first purchase experience in the customer's mind. Sure, they've invested their time hoping that you could help them be more effective, but they haven't voted with their wallets yet. And regardless whether someone buys a $15 ecommerce item or begins a monthly recurring service subscription worth $150,000 annually, crossing the payment threshold is a critical moment. There's now trust, either in the form of sharing credit-card details and forming a critical impression of your order handling, or in the continuing value that your service delivers.

For example, imagine the first time Zappos convinces you or your significant other to buy shoes via ecommerce. Getting past the barrier of not trying them on (backed by a great return policy) and offering both an extended selection and ultra-aggressive pricing is a strong value proposition—and one that can change the way a shopper buys shoes.

When we map out this journey, it's critical to understand both the history and the desired outcome. We need the data surfaced throughout the acquisition process, and we should have a solid idea of what we're trying to sell if there are multiple options. Oftentimes, the history comes through in the form of a behavioral-driven activity score, and the product preference should be a result of well-orchestrated content strategy and some timely sales contact.

This is also a moment when we need to deeply understand our own business. If you've got a sales team that closes very well, you need to figure out how to route the maximum amount of qualified leads to them. If marketing closes the sale, you need a one-to-many version of the same exact process.

The good news is that the business driver stays the same: how do you qualify the best prospects and then deliver offers that drive conversion? Your journey maps are going to include different touchpoints and customer buying levers depending on how and to whom you're selling.

For the first-purchase path, our hypothetical B2B software company should be absolutely focused on channel orchestration. By beginning with the lead source knowledge they've built over time, the question becomes what combination of marketing and sales programs reliably convert prospects into customers? Do you require a sales resource to close every deal over $1,000 or can a prospect educate themselves and move easily into the purchase phase? Determining what's most efficient for your business, and whether you spend more money on salespeople or website builds are key questions this analysis should answer.

Path to Repeat Purchase

If the path to first purchase is your chance to turn awareness into revenue, then this step represents the ability to architect an extremely profitable relationship over time. Lots of marketers I work with think of this in its most complicated format: a loyalty program. I've written extensively on loyalty and I have led retention marketing practices at Big 5 digital agencies, and I would contend almost any marketer can embrace the concepts of world-class loyalty programs without the astronomical costs associated with most.

First, I recommend some good old-fashioned regression analysis within your customer purchase data to determine the organic baseline for how often your customers currently buy. Assume this number is driven by the whole of your multichannel marketing effort, and in my experience more than 85 percent of marketers don't have specific programs to drive repeat purchase over time at the customer level. (If you're one of the rare ones who do, just make sure to factor your current programs into the baseline you've built—it just means you're going to have to work a bit harder to drive lift.)

There are also many scenarios where you won't have historical data to even run regression analysis. Maybe your company is brand new, or all your purchase data is locked up in an old ecommerce system. Regardless of the problem's source, here's where the art of marketing comes into play.

Scour your competitive landscape for purchase data. Spend time with market and financial analysts trying to understand sales cycles and revenues of similar businesses. If you're a new firm selling security software to businesses, understand how that spend fits into the rest of their technology stack. You're going to have to make an educated guess at a baseline number, so gather up as much raw information as possible and simply make the call.

Along with making the baseline assumption, you need to be focused on tracking the correct data points that will lead to clear benchmarks in the future. Maybe this means enhancements to your commerce tools or new reports from finance, but capturing the data in a usable format is the single most important tactic in this phase.

When it comes to mapping out the key journeys here, think deeply about three key elements: channel delivery, your cost-to-serve model, and revenue per transaction. In many cases, your path to first purchase will involve more resources and time than the second, third, or fourth purchase. And the combination of your costs and expected revenue should provide very clear guideposts on how best to sell.

For example, if you're an ecommerce seller of commodity items (books, sporting goods, toys, etc.), that means more up-front customer nurturing and convincing someone you're both price competitive and easy to buy from. In this case, your repeat purchase path should focus on architecting great offers to customers based on their behaviors that highlight purchase intent. A business traveler who bought a rolling carry-on suitcase from you six months ago may well show up again looking for a larger bag for an international trip. When you capture that browsing behavior, having an automated program running that delivers preferred customer pricing can be pure gold.

Conversely, if you're selling higher-dollar services to business buyers, this means you'll invest a lot of people time in presales activity to get to first purchase. Your journey map should factor for all the postsale touchpoints such as support and services to ensure satisfied customers who will renew their annual contracts. And you'll also want to factor for four to five sales touches throughout the year to both check customer satisfaction and maybe even begin an upsell conversation. It takes a ton of skill to be successful at scale, but you should be thinking about how to move direct, high-touch buyers to an increasingly self-service model.

Although these three key journeys are the most important, I know many marketers who architect journey maps for many more expected customer actions. For example, there's a postpurchase, first-support-call journey, or a subscription renewal journey. All these critical customer moments can and should be designed at this level of detail but bandwidth is always a challenge.

The good news is I've seen hundreds of marketers become increasingly more successful in this discipline. The benefits are almost always twofold: increased revenue with the same resources (an excellent outcome by itself), and much smarter deployment of resources to grow the revenue (paid media spend becomes conversion-driven, not someone's opinion).

Again, this is not a competency that's built overnight—or hired in with two new staffers—but it's based on a relatively simple four-step process. The preceding sections focused on what a great journey map contains, but consider the next section as your road map on how to arrive at great journey maps.

Four Steps to Greatness

Instead of always taking orders from your marketing or business colleagues, the behavioral-driven marketer is mapping out multistep interactions over time designed to support the buyer's intent. We're not spending eight hours testing the color or drop shadow on our buy button. We're not cutting new Excel lists that we upload each time we need to send a message. Yes, we care about optimizing each individual message, but more goodness is driven from mapping out the overall customer journey and designing campaigns to make the experience as frictionless as possible.

My most successful marketers set aside three to four days per month to think deeply about campaigns and strategy, as opposed to staying on the treadmill of execution. This time is typically spent on four key actions: (1) data analysis; (2) meeting with business and marketing stakeholders; (3) defining new programs; and (4) optimizing existing programs. Let's take a deeper look at each of these:

1. **Data analysis:** One of the key drivers of understanding is the data you have access to. It might be something as "big picture" as looking at your web analytics or marketing-automation platform tracking to understand where your web visitors are getting hung up. Think of each of those stopping or abandon points as opportunities to craft an automated program to help the user.

   For example, if you see an increased traffic on a specific product, but don't see a parallel increase in purchase actions, ask yourself what's missing. That would be a great moment to kick out a two-touch browse abandon program designed to test a unique value proposition or discount to see if you can drive the visitor to purchase.

   The same level of analysis should be applied to your own campaign performance metrics. How are your messages performing in terms of simple KPIs like opens and clicks? Is your multiple message interaction remaining constant during multistep programs indicating your audience is finding strong value in your content? Is your customer reactivation program effectively rescuing 8–10 percent of the people who qualify?

   The bottom line is that you need to get comfortable taking in data points, and building educated hypotheses based on them. Do not get hung up on needing bullet-proof evidence before acting. At the same time, don't be rash or overly quick to kill a program that doesn't bring in results right away.

My most successful marketers look at data to define potential testing approaches. When you truly embrace this way of thinking, you'll find more opportunity than you can ever take advantage of. Decide which of the solutions represent the clearest path to increased revenue or a better customer experience, and go hard on two to three solutions a quarter.

2. **Stakeholder relationships:** Although no one wants more meetings, most marketers could stand to be more in sync with their internal stakeholders. Understanding their success criteria and major business challenges allows you to increase your net value to them. And when you deliver value, the trust factor rises and typically everyone is more successful.

   If you're in a pure digital marketing role, it's critical to understand your business at a deep level. And I don't mean face-value things like product information and pricing—I mean comprehending your product-level cost-of-goods (so you can understand how much margin could be given away in discounting) and understanding how your multichannel sales processes work (so you can map the buyer's journey and match it to key marketing and sales moments).

   If you're in more of a customer relations management (CRM) role in which marketing is your primary customer (as opposed to the business side), you need to be the reference source on data quality, contact depth, and segmentation. Your marketers are going to look to you for segment-level insights and specific customer counts. You may well be asked to target a segment such as multiple-purchase customers in a specific city in a specific age range with a customer lifetime value (CLV) over $600. Or—if you're really killing it—you're going to them with these opportunity segments to discuss customer contact strategies and selling opportunities.

3. **Building new programs:** All the analysis and meetings don't mean jack unless you're building and deploying new programs that

address issues in the customer journey. Maybe your campaign is a short-term fix ahead of bigger web-based changes that will address the real problem, or maybe it's an epic cart abandon program that drives $750,000 a quarter by solving a real customer problem.

For example, I've worked with an ecommerce-based travel site who drives more than $1M a quarter with very well done cart abandon emails based on an average trip purchase in the $2,500 range. Once they understood how effective this behavioral marketing program was at capturing all-new revenue, they looked at other customer sticking points in the buying process.

They realized that a very normal and critical step in the buying process was the discussion between spouses about when and where they wanted to go. Typically, the user would spend time searching the site for locations and pricing, and assemble sample itineraries. Maybe it was comparing two to three Caribbean islands or deciding between Rome and Paris, but there was a natural browsing behavior before someone got serious.

Once their users began moving down the purchase path in the ecommerce platform, they were showing strong buying indicators. If the potential buyers didn't move all the way to purchase, they'd offer to email a PDF itinerary directly to the browser as a last-step rescue strategy. Of course, that email featured a very prominent buy-now button.

And guess what? That email converted at over 15 percent and drives more than $500,000 of top-line revenue every quarter. Why? Because it's brilliantly simple—it captures the buyer's intent and immediately provides a solution to the very real human problem that prevented the initial conversion.

So don't hesitate to build and deploy new programs that get to the heart of customer sticking points. They might end up just being a really smart customer touchpoint that your customer

appreciates—or it might drive half a million dollars in new revenue. You won't know until you execute.

4. **Optimize your existing programs:** Once you set up an abandon
   or reactivation campaign that works well, it begins to influence how
   you think about almost all your marketing efforts. When you think
   behavioral first, it's tempting to spend time making more and more
   programs, but keeping your existing programs sharp is critical.

   For example, many brands that have an unfortunate email
   delivery incident (like hitting the Spamhaus list or catching a
   blacklist at Gmail) undertake a manual list scrub to get back on the
   right track. It's typical to look at open statistics, and segment a list
   back to openers in the last 6 to 12 months—and then begin a slow,
   deliberate road back to solid deliverability.

   My counsel is always to build an automated program that achieves similar results so they don't find themselves back in that tough
   spot. Best practices today call for an always-on program that enfor-
   ces a 12-month (or less), zero-interaction policy on your database.
   When a recipient reaches those milestones (and maybe a few more
   such as no purchases or warranty registrations and a CLV of less
   than $50), they're immediately moved out of all mass-distribution
   lists into a specialized multistep nurture program designed to
   reactivate them. Most marketers think in terms of a three- or four-
   step program with about two weeks of space between communications. Each message should have an elevated degree of importance
   (and offer, if that's appropriate for your business). Many of the final
   messages I see simply ask the recipient to click one button as a
   minimum viable action. If they don't, add them to a separate suppression list (different from your primary opt-out list), and incor-
   porate that new list as the final step in all your queries.

   To further illustrate the point of optimizing programs: what
   drives this reactivation could clearly change by user type or buying
   season or as your own customer-facing value proposition changes.

Do not leave these automated programs running for months at a time without revisiting the creative and segmenting rules. In fact, go ahead and put a recurring meeting in your calendar reminding you to pull and analyze the KPI reports for the automated messages. Every once in a while I hear a marketer's horror story about an automated program they assumed was going along perfectly that hadn't been delivered in three months due to file name changes or other alterations that renders the automated program inoperable. Yikes!

So whether you've experimented with top-level journey mapping or if that still remains on your to-do list, the most important takeaway is to focus on reorienting your effort around the customer. Again, it's an easy thing to say—and an often harder thing to do. It requires us to break old product-focused habits and get out of our comfort zone.

But this is precisely what our customers want and need from us. I often remind marketers that their direct competitor is rarely the benchmark by which they're measured. Many customers' buying experience is baselined by Amazon, and their most used app is often the source of very timely notifications of friends joining.

The bottom line is buyers who receive hundreds of marketing communications daily have grown to expect those touchpoints to be relevant, timely, and to contain clear calls to action. And guess how they vote? With their time and their wallets.

So give them an equal amount of time and effort in the form of understanding their needs and wants. By laying out the specific tasks they're trying to achieve at each step in the process—and mapping those tasks back to your organization—almost every marketer I know has seen revenue growth. The simple act of increasing the relevance of your marketing will drive revenue in ways that small-scale content optimization or your legacy approach just can't reach.

8 Channel-Level Planning

Delivering Insane Relevance Every Time

As an evangelist for Silverpop, I travel like an unadulterated fool. I see an average of just over 100 customers face-to-face annually, typically in their offices, and in three- to four-hour sessions with the entire marketing team. I live in Atlanta, so this requires me to get on a Delta jet extraordinarily often; usually I rack up about 180,000 Sky-Miles a year. So you can imagine the breadth of my relationship with Delta Airlines.

I am the epitome of the multichannel user of Delta's offerings. On any given day I'm liable to open the iPhone app, dial up the call center, buy a ticket via my corporate travel portal or interact with Delta's Twitter-based customer service reps. To call me channel schizophrenic would be a radical understatement. The good news for me—and for Delta's business—is that they understand channel mix, and they do a nice job of eliminating friction out of many of my channel interactions.

As a simple example, the interactive voice response (IVR) system auto-recognizes my caller ID number and greets me by name and loyalty level. From there, I'm routed to the correct group of reps (with an expedited hold time), who greet me by name again, and who have all my booked itineraries up on their screen. In most cases, Delta is beginning to answer my question with a real human within 90 seconds of me dialing the 800 number. That's pretty well tuned.

So let's look at the various channels we as marketers have at our disposal to influence the buying process. Each has its own strengths and weaknesses that can range greatly across different industries, and each comes with its own cost of operations. As you'll see in the coming sections, understanding the cost implications versus the revenue potential is critical for defining how and when to invoke a channel-level tactic.

For the purposes of this conversation, we're going to focus on the channels in the following list. You may have more tricks in your marketing bag or you may have some of these still on your to-do list. Either way, the goal is to optimize what you have to factor for customer behaviors and make steady, solid progress toward increased revenue and customer satisfaction.

1. Email
2. Direct mail
3. Sales
4. Call center
5. Social media
6. Mobile applications

Email

Let's begin the conversation about channels with the most important and mature channel in your behavioral marketing world—email. Contrary to the three or four blog posts we all see annually that declare "email is dead," email still plays a critical role in the behavioral conversation. In fact, for many email is *the* channel of conversation across the entire marketing spectrum. A well-timed, relevant email probably does more to drive buying behavior than almost any other marketing touch point. Email is highly automated, can be done with an incredible personal touch, and has great economies of scale as a relatively inexpensive but strong-performing marketing channel.

It's important to remember that email is a very mature channel. We've had commercial email marketing in our toolbox for at least 8 to 10 years, which means that our teams and thinking have (hopefully) gotten very good.

But that doesn't mean every email approach is created equal. Many marketers think about using email only in a "batch and blast" type of world. Sending the same message to your entire audience certainly has some application for specific business cases, but it's not the way most successful marketers think about their marketing mix and how to optimize channels.

The beauty of email beyond its scale is to view highly automated email as a conversation. Within the last three to four years, we've seen the concept of nurture marketing rise to the level that it's greatly contributing to our online sales and successful relationships. No longer is a simple marketing email about the same topic as everyone else's received as relevant conversation. And with today's CRM tools powering many channels of interaction with our customers, we can collect unprecedented amounts of data.

Customers view of the exchange value for giving us this information (at a minimum) is that we provide them with an incredibly relevant email experience. Our role is, therefore, to focus on deepening our customer knowledge and being able to support effective sales and service opportunities when our customers need us.

The Power of Automation

One element that makes email such an effective channel is that we're able to effectively segment our customers and deliver clear nurtured journeys toward their desired outcome. Unlike other channels like social networks, in which a personal touch is a virtual requirement, email allows us to map out a three- or four-touch program that hits some really high-level points in a buyer's journey and effectively helps the multichannel process close business.

Consider a clothing retailer. For the last five or six years, most retailers have been focused on driving the maximum amount of traffic to their online stores. Some retailers undertook heavy discounting strategies. Others made the brand—and the selection of products that the brand offered—the differentiating factor.

Many retailers understand exactly how much revenue they can drive by sending a mass specific offer to their audience. They know, for example, that 25 percent of their audience will open a message on any given day, and 10 percent of them will click, which will net them approximately 2 percent conversion rate and roughly $7,000 in revenue. If the revenue target this month is $49,000, then they'll likely send seven campaigns. If one of the campaigns underperforms, there will likely be an eighth campaign, and so on.

This is how many brands end up with decreasing open rates, even lower click rates, and general list fatigue. These negative aspects of high-volume email marketing—specifically, deliverability issues in the form of blacklists and other delivery problems—are the strongest argument against batch-and-blast marketing. Once your lists begin aging and customer interactions decrease, you begin to risk both automated suppression (Hotmail and Google diverting your messages to the SPAM folder) and actual human suppression in the form of opt-outs and SPAM reports, which Internet service providers (ISPs) take incredibly seriously. If we do find ourselves at this point in the process, it takes a heroic effort to repair the deliverability and trust behind our email program.

Another more progressive view of how email supports the customer journey is to think about multitouch nurture programs. We deliver these kinds of campaigns to specific segments of our audience who are displaying *actual* behaviors over *specific* periods of time. This type of nurture marketing was pioneered primarily in the B2B space. Marketers understood that effectively selling long-lead, high-dollar items would require them to maintain a conversation with a prospect over time, and be able to modify their marketing and purchase messaging during that buyer's journey.

Silverpop provides a good example of how this nurture marketing has been traditionally used. We would undertake a series of content- and thought leadership-driven exercises that included everything from hundreds of blog posts a year to more than 50 branded events on an annual basis. All this effort focused on discovering new prospects, and understanding where they are in the buying process. Once someone comes into our database, the first line of action is a multitouch nurture program that begins to help us understand if someone is close to purchase or is truly only seeking educational information.

There are countless statistics around how much of the buying cycle is complete before prospects talk to vendors, and in many cases for a deeply considered purchase that number can easily be above 60 percent. So think about that: our customers already know almost everything about our product or solution before ever speaking to us. Clearly this means we'd better have architected an intelligent conversation that highlights our strengths and competitive advantage before someone calls our sales rep to make that purchase.

That exact dynamic is increasingly more common in e-commerce circles as well. Instead of using a specific lead score level or a demo request like a B2B process would, we look for purchase intent in other behaviors. A common action that many marketers have leveraged successfully is cart abandon. This program is routine among almost any ecommerce retailer of scale precisely because it translates the customer action of almost buying into real revenue.

Think about the last time you considered buying a new product or upgrading an existing service—like I did recently with Comcast. They have a well-timed cart abandon email that understands both the products and services I'm considering. So when I put new cable boxes in my cart to see the monthly pricing totals, they wait a couple of hours and send a reminder that I didn't actually finalize the purchase (as shown in Figure 8.1).

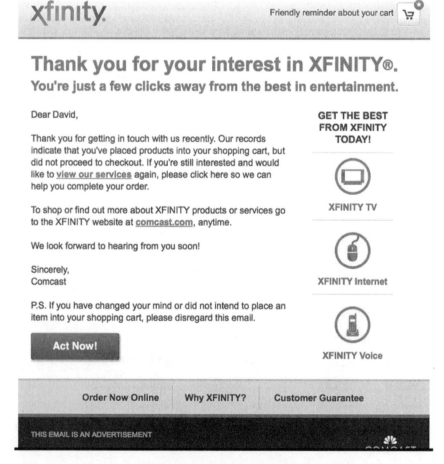

Figure 8.1 Comcast Cart Abandon Email Campaign

Although there are lots of content and offer strategies you can ply in a cart abandon email, I always counsel my marketers not to begin with a discount. Today's best practices point toward a two- to three-touch nurture campaign that begins within an hour of the abandon with a subtle reminder, and likely doesn't offer a discount until the final contact approximately a week later. As we move to a more stored payment-driven world, it's conceivable that redeeming a cart abandon offer might be limited to placing your thumb on the home button of your iPhone and paying with your card on-file with iTunes. Either way, this is a standard, must-do technique for ecommerce retailers in this day-and-age.

Batch-and-Blast in Its Rightful Place

When talking with marketers, I often use the analogy of using a different set of muscles to embrace behavioral marketing. We're seeking to build longer, deeper relationships with our customers, which calls for tactics beyond today's batch-and-blast email.

The reality for many marketers today—particularly those in ecommerce or who have a purchase-related call-to-action in their email content—is that batch-and-blast works—but typically only in the short term. If you've spent the time and energy to build a list larger than half a million or so, you can approximate pretty accurately how much revenue you'll drive when you hit send to everyone on your list.

I even know marketers who contend that all sales rise on big send days, which is likely attributed to *dark conversions*—a term used to describe transactions that just aren't being tracked accurately. Let's say that an email offer reminds a customer that they need to purchase a gift. But they're just leaving work, so they direct visit the site on their iPad and buy the item after they arrive home. They didn't literally click through from the email to track the purchase (and maybe your multi-device cookie strategy needs some work), but they did end up giving you money. However, your reporting doesn't show the campaign attribution in this scenario.

So even though there's easy money out there, the batch-and-blast methodology has an ugly side. In almost every case I see, this approach wears out customer goodwill, reduces response rates and conversions over time, and can end up creating major deliverability issues. It's also typically hit-and-miss with relevance to each individual recipient, which leads to a whole host of other issues.

This approach still has a place in your communications mix; but odds are you'll notice those campaigns becoming your weakest performers if you're tracking and reporting well. If you're similar to my average digital marketers, typical open rates will grind down to below 15 percent, and your conversion will hover just below 1 percent.

That's not to say they don't drive great top-line revenue; 1 percent of 20 million is still a lot of cash. But layering in behavioral-driven campaigns like cart abandon will demonstrate what it's like to have an open rate of 40 percent+ and a conversation rate about 15 percent.

Direct Mail

Of all the channels we discuss in this section, I'm convinced that direct mail might be the most underestimated trick in most marketers' bags. You've likely either grown up (professionally) in a world that was heavily direct mail or you haven't ever tackled it at all. Its inherent complexity (external vendors abound) and cost mean that most marketers don't proactively add this to their channel mix. It also doesn't help that it enjoys a less-than-positive sentiment that always focuses on how expensive it can be.

Although it's true that postage costs are an ever-rising issue, and competing with the noise level and/or the ignore factor within someone's physical mailbox is an equal challenge, reaching out to a highly valued (or qualified) customer as part of a true multichannel buying experience can be very powerful. Just think about how many catalogs you receive in the mail. If that model didn't work, you'd stop getting them in under a month.

So there really are two key use cases for great direct mail. The first is a traditional catalog marketer, which is a role many digital marketers could learn a few key lessons from. For catalogers, the ability to grow a list is uninhibited by pesky little rules like opt-in permissions. Sure you might have to deal with do-not-mail lists, but the penalties take the form of your wasted printing costs—not $10,000 per message fines from the Federal Trade Commission.

When the size of your audience is not limited by outside regulatory influences, the economics of marketing come into play—making three questions rather clear:

1. How big can I get my list?
2. What's my strategy for uncovering active buyers?
3. How much am I willing to spend to drive one average transaction?

You might notice that these questions are not radically different from how the smartest behavioral marketers might view the world: we care about scale, cost, and return. We're numbers driven and are both tracking and acting on customer behaviors at scale. Interestingly, I see some very strong catalog brands take to behavioral marketing very quickly. Because they already think in segments, actions, and cost, converting that from physical catalogs to digital communications is likely easier.

For example, I've spent a fair amount of time with a European holding company that owns multiple brands in a specific Benelux country. Their business consists of multiple market segments such as grocery, home, and baby—much of which they market in very traditional ways (catalog, outdoor, etc.). It'd be as if their country's version of IKEA, Kroger, and Babies "R" Us were all under the same corporate umbrella.

At one point, someone mentioned that the overwhelming majority of households in the country were somewhere on their house lists. Interestingly, they're an absolutely brilliant catalog marketer for all their nongrocery businesses and are perfectly comfortable with SKU variations by zip code, customer lifetime value (CLV), and other deep-stack tactics. So while they adopt behavioral marketing at a slower pace than your average ecommerce startup—because they can afford to grow slow and steady—it's the discipline of their heritage that gives them a huge leg up.

The genesis of the first lesson behavioral marketers can take from great direct mailers is to understand the cost-driven metrics of marketing. Oftentimes it's easy to think of email as free and to, therefore, be willing to blast everything to everyone. However, almost every marketer comes to see how the 80/20 rule comes into play here: that is, at least 80 percent of the interactions and spend come from the top 20 percent of active recipients. I have ecommerce brands who regularly drive 40 percent+ of their email revenue from less than 3 percent of their send volume. So think about how you market more effectively to a smaller audience to drive greater results.

The second lesson direct mail offers is cross-channel activation. As much as we'd love to believe everything happens in digital—and it primarily does for our youngest audience members—the challenge is often more about creating a strong multichannel campaign that performs better than a single channel could alone.

For example, imagine you're a very smart ecommerce marketer who understands CLV deeply, but you're working on making your email program more effective. That lack of email prowess is likely costing you high-dollar opt-outs in the course of your normal marketing efforts. Perhaps you should consider building customer-specific rescue programs that run completely via direct mail. Although we don't want to double-down on annoying a customer post opt-out, a simple follow-up survey sent via postcard might be just what you need to restart the conversation—or at least figure out what you're doing wrong that's costing you subscribers.

Although that's the "save case," you might also think about direct mail as a great way to deepen your presales relationship in a complicated, long-cycle sales environment. In this day and age, there's probably an equal chance this could be a B2B or B2C scenario.

Sending direct mail offers to luxury automobile buyers is a tried-and-true method for driving existing brand loyalty, new brand consideration, and traffic into retail dealerships. The same scenario works if you're selling health insurance products on behalf of registered agents to employers with more than 500 staff members. Understanding that each employer reviews prices and features in the second quarter to determine their offerings for the next calendar year presents an excellent opportunity for marketing to send a "meeting-maker" campaign designed to identify high-value prospects who are ready to buy. A beautifully well-orchestrated meeting-maker program has the opportunity to drive 5 to 10 times the revenue over the program costs if it features a strong offer and great audience segmentation.

Direct mail can be a great second-channel play in support of a solid digital strategy. Although there are still industries that are direct mail first (think couponing), many of those will likely become digitized over the next three to five years. There's a very clear business-model reason that the United States Postal Service is now delivering packages on Sundays for Amazon: less and less of their revenue will come from postage.

One last item to consider is direct mail's powerful ability to aggressively prospect for new customers without the restrictions that come with phone or email. Although you can buy names for fractions of a penny, the conversion rate into truly loyal customers is normally minuscule. Depending on the product or service you're selling, this type of carpet-bombing prospecting might make sense. If it does, understand its limitations and know that it's probably not sustainable as your only method of customer targeting.

Sales

Although there are literally thousands of books on sales processes, sales strategies, and sale technologies, this section focuses on two very clear behavioral-driven moments:

1. When to invoke sales.
2. How to arm sales with as much data as possible.

Some of this thinking will vary based on your industry or business model, but I'll present the overall concepts in enough depth that it will be easy to apply them to your particular world.

First, let's look at another example based on Silverpop's internal thinking about how sales fits into the ideal behavioral-marketing-driven buying experience. Before we start, one caveat: Silverpop's business is a pure-play software-as-a-service (SaaS) model that relies on a one-to-many, marketing- and content-driven process to fill the top of the prospect funnel. It's different than a traditional services-driven model such as a consultancy that depends on successful projects run by on-site resources that then lead to bigger projects with the same (or similar) customers. I'll focus on the SaaS model as it neatly delineates the roles of marketing, inside sales, and outside sales.

In a world of fully realized behavioral marketing, it's not difficult to define—and even quantify—the roles of the marketing and sales. Marketing's primary function is to produce two key deliverables: leads and content. Marketing is top-of-the-funnel in a pure SaaS world and has the job of delivering an ever-increasing volume of qualified leads to the sales function.

As a result, marketing should be managing a wide variety of programs such as corporate-branded events, external sponsorships, digital advertising (banners, search, etc.), and deeply specific nurture programs by customer and lead type. Behind this lead-driving machine, most solid marketers have a scoring system that exists to separate the proverbial wheat from the chaff. When a prospect's score rises high enough from marketing's activities, they're considered a marketing qualified lead (MQL) and passed over to inside sales.

Inside sales' job is to run a progression with the newly minted sales qualified lead (SQL)—which is just a fancy term for what happens when sales takes ownership of the lead from marketing. In most cases, the first effort is to close the business without involving outside sales in order to keep acquisition costs lower. If the marketing function can't close the business directly, then it's inside sales' job to gather additional information (demographic, buying authority, product needs, etc.) in order to power the best possible outcome for outside sales.

In some cases, inside sales will receive leads that are qualified but not ready to buy. Maybe they're the right industry and company size, but still have six months left on a contract with your competitor. Or maybe they're studying up to understand the next level of service provider that can support their business when growth takes off. Regardless of the reason, this is the magic moment for inside sales to either accelerate the lead to outside sales for full pursuit, or decelerate the lead into a marketing-driven nurture program that's ideally industry- and/or buyer-need based.

This happens frequently in the Silverpop marketing effort. We'll meet a prospect at an event or conference, and they'll just be starting to shop for next year's vendor. They might not be ready to sign on the dotted line next month, but by delivering a well-executed, informative nurture program, we earn the right to be considered during the next buying cycle.

Profile	Behavior					
	1	**2**	**3**	**4**		
A	Target Fit Heavy Interest	Target Fit Some Interest	Target Fit Unclear Intent	Target Fit Low Activity	Sales Team	
B	Potential Fit Heavy Interest	Potential Fit Some Interest	Potential Fit Unclear Intent	Potential Fit Low Activity	Demand Gen	
C	Insufficient Info Heavy Interest	Insufficient Info Some Interest	Insufficient Info Unclear Intent	Insufficient Info Low Activity	Marketing/ Nurture	
D	No Info Heavy Interest	No Info Some Interest	No Info Unclear Intent	No Info Low Activity		

Figure 8.2   Graph on Outside Sales

We cannot overstate how critical this point is in your lead process. Everything else in the marketing and sales process should be built to optimize this moment. If too many are decelerating to nurture programs, you need to improve your lead capture sources. If everyone's being passed along to outside sales, it's time to evaluate your inside sales decision-makers and look closely at the lead-to-close percentages.

Figure 8.2 should begin to illuminate how we answer the "when" question for sales—and how we factor for both marketing and demand generation as well. In order to maintain everyone's sanity, I almost always suggest you turn on scoring functionality across your processes. Having an objective number that determines when a lead is passed from marketing to sales (and back, if necessary) has some very important benefits, including these:

- Marketing understands (and can be measured by) the importance of spend versus quality.
- Sales understands the marketing touch points that lead to the high score.
- Executive management can look at a holistic, end-to-end sales process and understand where to make additional investments.
- Trust and confidence are built among the entire leadership team.

This helps take emotions and personalities out of the equation. Either marketing is delivering high-quality leads based on a reasonable budget, and sales is closing a logical number of deals or they're not, and you need to hold someone accountable.

Before we discuss what data needs to flow to sales to power the right outcomes, let's look at scoring for a minute. We talk in detail about scoring throughout the book, so a real-life example about how scoring can bring customer understanding to life is helpful here.

One of our customers in the home security space implemented a top-to-bottom scoring model designed to further segment their leads into hot, warm, and cold prospects. Following much historical research on response rates and conversion numbers, they defined six major key attributes in two top-level categories on which to base scores. In almost every case, I'd recommend focusing on their top-two categories: demographic and behavioral. These two elements nicely combine the "who" and "what" actions we're trying to get at.

Within demographic and behavioral, their analysis pointed out three key decision-making elements:

1. **Demographic**

   a. Home ownership: Given the purchase was a long-term investment, they discovered homeowners bought more often, even though they had a relatively unique value proposition for renters. The values they assigned were a simple 200 for homeowners, and 50 for renters.

   b. Credit score: With thousands of dollars of equipment installed up front and a multiyear contract, it was important to focus on customers who would pay regularly. The values assigned ranged from 300 for excellent to a low of 15 for a sub-600 credit score.

   c. Lead generation source: They had a referral model that involved incentives for both the referrer and referee, and sometimes also featured specific collateral materials for the new prospect. When

the collateral was involved, the conversion rate went up significantly so they assigned 200 points to that action, and a low of
25 points to someone who was a simple web or phone lead.

2. Behavioral

a. Clicks on buy now links: This is one of the very clear buying
indicators, and they immediately assigned 200 points to any user
who took this action. For clicks on other links within the mail
content, they'd assign 100 points to factor for a positive interaction—but not all the way to full-on buying behavior.

b. Visits to website purchase pages: They had specific scoring
moments set for multiple pages on the site, including a landing
page that lived at www.example_site.com/buynow, which earned
the user 100 points. Any other page visit earned the user
100 points for each page visited.

c. Opening email: In addition to follow-on actions that indicated
buying behavior, they also wanted to positively factor for people
who were interacting often with their nurture programs. So for
each email open, every user was assigned 15 points.

As you can see, this model actively selects for specific persona-level
buyers who are taking purchase-like behaviors.

An absolutely critical overlay to all these event-based scores is the
concept of time. The company clearly understood that, more often,
buyers convert early and through the middle of a typical buying cycle
(90 days in their case). To adequately factor for time, they assigned one-
time scores to users at the beginning of a time period—100 for the first
three days, 75 for days four to seven, 25 for the first month, and so on
down to 90 days.

And because they clearly understood very few people bought after
90 days, they added what I refer to as a "top-kill" value of –5,000
assigned to the 91st day. This effectively erased virtually all prospects
from the model given that the average high score in the model was

between 2,500 and 3,000. This is a pretty heavy-handed tactic, but I applauded them for being data-driven enough to know when to expend their resources on another user who is more likely to close.

Once they had mapped out and began tracking all these individual scores, it was time to validate a ranking model. The process of ranking each of these scores against the others is critical in building relevance between each of the prospects—since it helped marketing decide which segments to double-down on in terms of additional content and offers, and highlighted which segments had a low probability of converting.

Their model allowed them to individually rank each customer based on their actual behaviors, and the tiers looked like Figure 8.3.

Finally, they allowed the model to run for four to six weeks, and then calculated conversions based on the scores each user achieved. This generated a conversion rate for each of the ranks shown in Figure 8.3, and in this case, clearly highlighted that the A's and B's were the sweet spot of conversion. It wasn't a surprising result, but imagine the clarity with which they can now market to hot prospects. The brand has unequivocal evidence of which scores predict conversion.

Ranking

				Edit | Clear
A+	is greater than or =	2000 Points		
A	is between	1500 Points	and	1999 Points
B+	is between	1000 Points	and	1499 Points
B	is between	750 Points	and	999 Points
B-	is between	500 Points	and	749 Points
C	is between	250 Points	and	499 Points
D	is between	100 Points	and	249 Points
F	is less than or =	99 Points		

Figure 8.3 Graph on Customer Ranking

Simply focusing on those most likely to convert earned them thousands more in revenue and invaluable customer insight. And by later separating their highest performing A and B segments into even more granular segments including A+, B+, and B-, they were able to almost triple the conversion rates in each audience group.

And what are their secret weapons in converting the A's and B's at an ever-increasing rate? You're spot-on if you guessed hot leads being dropped directly into inside sales call queues. A fully objective scoring model running behind the scenes, combined with a well-trained inside sales function, was exactly what they needed to take revenue to the next level.

So if invoking sales at the perfect moment is an early step toward greatness, the question then becomes: what data does that salesperson need to close quickly and effectively? Simply throwing names and phone numbers over the proverbial wall will be an exercise in futility—particularly for the prospect. They don't want a call to rehash all the information they've already received and comprehended. And the sales resource doesn't want to dial blindly to what you're claiming is a hot prospect.

This is where a CRM system can serve as an important "connective tissue" system between marketing and sales. With the rise of fully SaaS-driven CRM platforms, it's not difficult to trial a few market leaders—like Microsoft Dynamics or NetSuite or Salesforce—to understand which works best for your business. Whichever option you choose will depend on a ton of different factors, but having technology to support this critical moment is a solid strategy for building toward your ideal future state.

Silverpop marketers are most likely to have all their email and marketing automation data bi-directionally synced with one of the CRM platforms mentioned above. A prospect is a known entity to both platforms, and salespeople's actions are all consolidated such that marketing and sales each have their own segmented but shared view of the customer relationship. For example, the Silverpop platform would hold all the campaign-level resources and response rates, and any new record-level data appending would probably be done in CRM.

The most critical set of data is what we call "customer insight"— simply a list of every campaign sent to the prospect. This allows sales to take a quick spin through everything a prospect has received to power a much more intelligent conversation. They now understand which whitepapers they've read, what pricing has been communicated, and so forth. That level of detail might power a call script something like this:

Hi Bryan, this is Jenny from Company X calling and I wanted to follow-up with you regarding our solutions. I know we've shared a few important whitepapers with you in the last three months—especially the one on buyer segmentation—and I'd like to see if you're ready to schedule a demo to see the platform in action? As you know from our Company Y case study, we have some great automotive industry solutions that could really drive your business. I've also got a handful of 30-day trial invites, and I'd be glad to share one with you.

Jenny has a clear understanding of multiple data points that keep this conversation productive and fast-paced:

1. She knows Bryan is an approved prospect with a score high enough to get him into her call queue.
2. She can see the exact whitepapers Bryan has received.
3. The next step in their ideal customer journey is a demo, which is Jenny's desired outcome during this call.
4. Jenny knows the industry segment of Bryan's company, and also knows he's consumed content related to it.
5. Jenny also knows Bryan's company has been approved to receive the free trial offer.

This type of cross-channel orchestration gives buyers subtle yet powerful indications you're paying attention and honing your marketing efforts. Even a subconscious advantage at this critical juncture is enough to tip the scales to conversion. Many times a highly informed, successful interaction is what pulls the buying moment forward to now.

Tying marketing and sales together around key customer behaviors is not always easy. However, it's one of the most powerful strategies you can employ if both groups actively sell your products or services. The cost of a phone call can be an expensive touch point, but by making sure that person is perfectly armed with all the previous contact details and any available offers creates a perfect buying opportunity for your prospect. The rep can dynamically deal with any product and/or company objections, and will have the opportunity to overtly ask for the sale. And sometimes that's all it takes—a well-orchestrated digital nurture process followed by an educated closing call.

Call Center

Although we've talked in-depth about how to integrate inside sales into your behavioral marketing efforts, it's important to factor for the times when you have less control over the entire process—namely, inbound call centers scenarios. Many of the same dynamics—including how to arm your reps with the maximum customer information—apply here, but in this case we need to take a fundamentally more progressive view of the call center's role.

There was a time in the late 1990s and early 2000s when call centers were outsourced to other places on the globe in order to cut costs. As customers' experiences degraded, they became increasingly dissatisfied and vocal—just as the rise of social media began. Remember the short-lived NBC sitcom *Outsourced* that ran for one season in 2010? If an aspect of marketing is so pervasive as to be lampooned in a sitcom, you *know* it's bad.

Old school marketers only ever saw call centers as a necessary (and really expensive) evil—something they had to offer to customers to keep them out of retail locations, and be able to deal with the scale of thousands of customers. Although there were some technology improvements over the years, the average cost per call never got much below approximately $7.50 with a decently trained U.S.-based call center. And when you extrapolate those costs over thousands or millions of customers, you can imagine how fast the costs get out of hand.

I worked internally for a market-leading package delivery company whose business operated at a scale few industries could match—imagine something on the order of 12 to 15 million packages a *day*. Each time a driver attempted delivery at a commercial address and no one was present to sign, they'd leave a small notice with the phone number and website information to schedule the next delivery attempt. Most times, though, the customer would simply call the main 800 number and have to navigate the interactive voice response (IVR) system to find the right call center rep. There was also a large volume of website home-page visits where package recipients were trying to solve the same problem.

The steady state of the daily volume ran around 20,000 calls into the call center. It slowly crept up over time, and when it reached about 50,000 calls per day, we'd deploy a full set of on-site assets including home page banners and customized landing pages. Within hours, it would drive the volume back down to ~20,000 calls a day, and the process would begin again. In that example, you can imagine the cost-savings impact of 30,000 fewer calls in the call center *per day*.

With that level of savings available, it's not surprising that companies of all shapes and sizes ended up shipping the call center overseas. The opportunity to cut out 66 percent of the cost was just too tempting for executives looking to wring every penny of cost out of the business.

Yet because the customer experience suffered greatly, there was a great deal of pressure on companies to return call centers to the United States. Unfortunately for many—but fortunate for the call center industry—the Great Recession of 2008 began to displace workers at large scale. And one of the emerging jobs for the hardest hit areas like rural North Carolina became U.S.-based call center representatives.

A few interesting things happened about the time these functions began to come back stateside. As mentioned previously, it took place just as social media was becoming more widely used—giving customers a much louder voice and larger audience to complain about a brand's shortcomings. Before Facebook, the biggest risk might be someone who wrote a letter to the editor that then actually got published—which was clearly not enough risk to modify any given company's subpar behavior.

At about the same time, the Recession decimated many consumers' spending power, prompting even more competition for every dollar spent. However, the smartest marketers realized that quality service could be a differentiator. Sure, everyone was going to have to be price-aggressive to retain their share of spend; but the ability to have a more personal customer interaction with a call center rep became a distinguishing factor.

We often see this in the travel industry; specifically, in how companies like Delta Air Lines and Hilton Hotels doubled down on their best customers with dedicated call center reps. But this also was a time when many manufacturer brands saw an opportunity to develop customer-facing relationships they'd previously left to the retail channels where they began. Many brands like Dyson, Graco, and Hoover were introducing (or expanding) their product registration and product warranty registration events to begin to build a customer database that could be both marketed or sold to in the future.

These "new-school" marketers began looking at every customer touch point as an opportunity to deepen the relationship. It's very powerful for a child-car-seat company like Graco to understand the age of my two daughters. The product registration event helps them comply with customer notification laws in the event of recall, but it also gives them some great clues about when my girls should be moving from convertible car seats to booster seats. And those critical data points—captured by a well-trained call center rep during a simple product registration call—could easily become the data behind the decision points on when to kick off dynamic marketing programs.

The key for inserting behavioral marketing into your inbound call center begins with the right sizing of your thinking on that overall touch point. Do you see it as an opportunity to deepen your customer relationship? Are you willing to train a small group in your call center to go beyond the basics? Could you cross-sell or cross-market other solutions to your customers?

If not, stop now and do nothing. The best next move is to assign a business analyst to do an ROI model for the entire channel, but, honestly, next year is probably fine in terms of timing. When you prove the business case, then begin slowly with rep training and data collection goals.

On the other hand, if you can highly value the touch point—and build a back-of-the-napkin business case that shows tens of thousands of dollars in cost savings—then it's time to get down to business! You'll begin saving money almost immediately on a per-call basis, and you can aggressively benchmark your data collection goals. Also, you'll want to factor a call center touch into your attribution models so you can understand how often that role contributes to closing business.

You might wonder why I'm so quick to write off behavioral marketing in an inbound call center without a 100 percent commitment. It has *nothing* to do with the cost savings or revenue upside, both of which are very strong in call centers. It's more about a marketer's capacity to execute.

If you're not absolutely committed to something as complex as reengineering a call center, it's a mistake to even begin the exercise. As a marketer, you'll need to work very closely with a much broader group of internal stakeholders and have built extensive trust in your ability to deliver. Most successful projects in this space are spearheaded by a VP or someone in a higher role—someone who has a virtually direct reporting line authority to key resources in hiring, training, and operations.

Social Networks

If an inbound call center is the optional place to take on behavioral marketing, then social networks are the other end of the spectrum: that is, you don't have a choice, and most of your competitors are already doing it. Although there are literally millions of words written annually on social media marketing and strategy, we're going to focus on how to make three to five key decisions about behavioral marketing and *your* strategy. Although they're fantastic examples of success in this area, what works for Starbucks, Arby's, and Delta Air Lines is not likely to be the best strategy for you.

It's critical to remember one important point regarding social channels: these channels require more human touch than any other pure marketing channel (excluding sales and the call center). Authenticity and a specific brand voice are not optional components. No matter how automated our listening tools that slice-and-dice user behaviors can become, the moment of person-to-person interaction had better be filled with context and continuity. If we're willing to excuse a brand's occasional dynamic email slip-up, there's zero room for error with Twitter replies or Facebook comments.

I see first-hand the effort it takes to manage social networks well among my customers. In general, marketers should spend about 30 hours per month per social network in order to truly win. Therefore, if one person at your company is running Facebook, Twitter, and LinkedIn as 50 percent of their job, it's safe to say things are not exactly optimized. There's likely a lot of cross-posting that might make activity numbers look great, but the next level of interactions is probably a pretty grim story. If you're not dialing interactions specifically for each audience, you could be doing much better. We'll talk more in-depth about voice later, but let's look at the three key issues you need to address as the basis for a great behavioral-driven social strategy:

1. Marketing versus listening
2. Brand versus customer support
3. Customer/prospect demographics versus existing networks

Listen or Market

First, there's a very legitimate question to answer right off the top: are you going to market at all? That may sound crazy, but if at least half your effort in social networks isn't listening, then you're missing the point.

Just so we're all on the same page, I'll define *listening* as the process of doing user-level research and building people-on-topic lists on any social network. And *marketing* is exactly what most people think of when undertaking social networks: content creation and engaging conversations that lead to interactions.

Let's look at a few examples where listening is significantly more important than marketing. Almost every business I work with has a steady stream of new products that—in a perfect world—are driven by customer demand. What better place than Twitter search could there be to plug in highly specific keywords and immediately see what a couple of hundred million people think about a specific topic? In addition, I know many marketers who do *highly* granular Facebook advertising to target 15 to 20 users for a focus group on new product innovation.

Another big reason to focus on social listening is to keep your finger on the pulse of customer satisfaction. Although there are a lot of vendors and agencies you can hire to do social listening at-scale, I often recommend marketers simply spend one day a month searching their brand and product names across all relevant social networks as a first step. See how and when people post about your brand. Think through the types of customer dialog your marketing is creating. Are others in your organization having two-way conversations? Or are unanswered complaints the norm?

Finally, taking time to listen to your customers via social networks simply makes you a better marketer. Understand the human side of what you're creating, and look for ways to be more relevant and personal. Another critical activity: take a deep look at what your top two to three competitors are doing in social networks. Look deeply at the full conversations behind their tweets originating from their main account. Do their customers consistently complain about pricing or uptime or something else? Or are there multiple-customer conversations praising their support and product teams?

Understanding the general social sentiment toward them is interesting data to have—or maybe you want to take social sentiment to a deeper, more algorithmic place and work with tools like Datasift or AlchemyAPI.

The bottom line is this: Is there a takeaway opportunity for a certain segment of users who are frustrated with your biggest competitor? Could you at least engage a small set of competitive users in a conversation that might sharpen your product strategy or marketing approach? If you're not regularly visiting twitter.com/search to look at relevant hash tags and conversations, add that to your to-do list today!

Whatever the industry, almost every marketer I know who steps outside their traditional daily activities of slamming campaigns and getting reports out the door finds some significant insight among all the data available through social listening.

On the other side of the spectrum is the traditional social media marketing that everyone's familiar with. Although the best practices are always changing—like today when Facebook and Twitter posts with both text and photos drive more clicks and interactions—the primary reason to engage with social networks is your customer's expectation.

Regardless of whether you like it, there are two dynamics at play among today's consumers:

1. **Presales research:** Because so much information is available online, consumers now dig deeper and understand more about almost any product than they would have five to seven years ago. They don't need a Best Buy sales rep to sell them refrigerators; they've already visited the manufacturer's site to decide which one they want, and researched warranties and read every model's review on *Consumer Reports*. All they want when visiting the store is to know who can get their specific unit in their home for the lowest price.

   Depending on whose statistics you believe, the percentage of decision can be as high as 70 percent before a customer ever engages with a seller. If you aren't meeting your prospects in social channels and engaging in presales conversations about features, pricing, availability, and lifestyle, you are *absolutely* missing the boat. It doesn't matter how much your product costs or where the consumer buys it; you need to interact with them early and often to drive purchase preference down the road.

2. **Social proof:** If the presocial Internet delivered all the stats, pricing, and product information to consumers, then the age of social channels has given rise to the idea of social proof. How many times have you seen friends or followers in your own social networks asking for recommendations or opinions on specific companies, products, or services? Just this week alone, I had a friend in Florida researching home alarm companies on Facebook; I posed a question to my Twitter followers about finding a new accountant; and my wife was buying items to make Valentine's Day cards for our daughter's preschool classmates she'd found on Pinterest.

   Think about your own behavior in this increasingly social world. How often have you gone to Amazon to read the reviews on an item you were preparing to buy at retail? If you're going to drop hundreds of dollars on a summer camp for your kids, how many people are you going to ask about it? The reality is we simply don't take service providers or sellers at their own word anymore because we don't need to. Having four of your friends confirm that a particular summer camp is awesome—even though it's $200 more than the one you were originally looking at—is what drives both the buying decision and the increased spend. Every single time.

For all the reasons just outlined, the "why" of social marketing should already be a done deal for most marketing departments. If you're still trying to convince management that social channels are important components, just go online. There are literally hundreds of case studies available; it's easy to find five to six in your industry or vertical and keep beating the drum. Driving very early conversations with your prospects and being able to demonstrate the value you bring is quickly becoming required table stakes in the selling process.

Brand or Support

Once we're past the "why," then it's time to figure out the "how" behind social media—and what types of behaviors are the true golden moments to focus on. To begin, this requires a fundamental understanding of your business—and what your customer is trying to achieve when they interact with you in social channels. Do they need reassurance that your brand of clothing most closely fits their lifestyle, or do they need you to rebook an airplane seat on a just-cancelled flight? These very different needs require a truly unique approach.

If you're a brand marketer whose job is to create buying preference over time through social interactions, then having a marketer managing your social feed is ideal. Keeping active audiences aware of new products, delivering new content, interacting with current and future customers are all great reasons to dive into your social networks of choice. Your goal should be to support your customer's information needs and to build more raving fans. You should be personally engaging in most discussions about your brand in a subtle, nonsales way. Be the conversation.

If, on the other hand, you're in the airline business, then your social channels are really just an extension of your customer support function. In this case, you need to have someone with call center skills and great social media awareness. You'll want to think through 24-hour coverage, and you should probably add the individual user's initials to the end of each tweet to keep conversations personalized and coordinated. (See the example from Delta Air Lines in Figure 8.4 showing both a tweet itself, and the background referring the two initials back to a first name and last initial, which beautifully humanizes the interaction.) From a behavior perspective, you should be focused on reducing customers' pain points. Many days that will be connecting flight information, weather updates, and destination details, but sometimes it's just thanking them for their business.

Figure 8.4 Screenshot of Delta Website

Your business is probably somewhere in the middle—and that is when it becomes challenging. The best marketers I work with build strong networks across their companies in which they delegate issues, and generally default to a more brand-driven social approach. They want to encourage interactions and conversations with both customers and prospects, but they have a clear plan to deal with complaints and scheduling issues.

One of the clearest points of delineation can be specific customer behaviors that you optimize your social channels to handle. One recent example is the rise of Twitter's advertising product called Lead Generation Cards. By reducing a user's action to a single "submit" click to opt-in to an email list, contest, or other program, Lead Generation Cards provide a low-effort way to get user-level information (typically email address and Twitter username) pumped directly into your marketing database so you can continue the conversation across other channels.

Some of the most progressive marketers also use a combination of outside vendors and API technology to understand user sentiment at-scale. Technology certainly exists to keep a running tally on whether someone has a positive, neutral, or negative opinion of you and/or your products, which can then be used to deliver dynamic content across other channels like email.

Regardless of which flavor of social you implement, you'll need to remain flexible in how you view the channel. Today's awareness-building efforts should migrate into deeper customer understanding goals over the next 12 to 18 months. Finding the right balance between service, support, and sales—all executed with a consistent, authentic voice—is a long-term goal that requires lots of different tactics along the way.

Which Social Networks

In a world of limited marketing resources, almost all of us have to make hard decisions about which social networks to focus our efforts on.

Facebook and Twitter were first for many brands, so there hasn't been much reallocation of effort for Instagram or Pinterest—even if they might provide radically better user interactions. You need to prioritize your social focus based on two key attributes: demographics and desired outcomes.

Look at your primary customer/prospect data from a demographic perspective, and map that to the age and gender of the top social networks. For me, the initial list should be:

- Facebook
- Twitter
- Instagram
- Pinterest
- LinkedIn
- Google+
- Vine
- Snapchat
- YouTube
- Tumblr
- Reddit
- Flickr

If you want to reach a mainly female audience in their 40s with lifestyle content that supports social buying proof, then Facebook is probably the right choice based on demographic. But be prepared to spend some real advertising dollars, given that organic (nonpaid) marketing has been severely hampered by the Facebook algorithms designed to keep the feeds of more than billion people somewhat manageable. A great secondary choice for the same demographic would be Pinterest; but remember that Facebook's objective of keeping up with friends is *radically* different than Pinterest's creative inspiration message. Although the audiences are similar, most marketers I know believe Pinterest is much more effective at driving direct ecommerce transactions and revenue than Facebook.

On the other end of the demographic spectrum, consider trying to reach 20- to 30-year-old technology-oriented men. In that case, choosing Twitter or Reddit are probably your best choices. Beginning in 2015, user data is showing Twitter moving away from its traditional 50/50 split among males and females, so doubling down on men on Twitter for lifestyle brands is probably a good move. Reddit, on the other hand, is a hugely active curated social news network that self-describes as "the front page of the Internet"—but is almost systemically allergic to marketing of any kind. To effectively manage Reddit, you'd better bring your superauthentic, nonsales hat every minute of every day. You must blend into this community, and be willing to add more value than you extract. If your idea of social marketing is cross-posting Twitter content on Facebook—complete with hashtags that mean nothing on Facebook—then avoid Reddit like the plague. You'll be glad you never got flamed out of existence.

Once we take the first pass on demographic matching, we then must ask the behavior question: that is, what do we want our customer or prospect to *do* as a result of our marketing efforts? If the answer is consume our content—and for instance, believe that we're an employer of choice because you are considering a job change—then LinkedIn should be your focus. If your goal is an ecommerce transaction, then go all-in on the quality of your product photos and focus on Instagram and Pinterest.

Remember, every social network you take on will require approximately 30 hours of effort each month—and will have its own unique content-creation requirements. Do *not* make the mistake of trying to do all of them with limited resources. Focus on demographics, key behaviors, and desired outcomes when choosing your two to four top priorities.

Author's Note: For the purposes of this section, I've referred to all these sites as social networks, which isn't 100 percent accurate. Although Facebook is a pure social network geared around you and your friends, Twitter is much more like a publishing platform where your followers are the digital equivalent of old-school subscribers, but there's a clear social element. And video-sharing sites like YouTube also serve more of a publishing function. However, there's even less focus on specific followers and the conversation is relegated to the comments section. You'll need to understand the true meaning of each service in order to make an educated decision about where to spend your limited time and money.

Mobile Applications

Finally let's look at the channel that likely has the most growth potential over the next 12 to 18 months: mobile applications.

To begin, ask yourself the fundamental question about this emerging channel. Do you view mobile apps as a necessary evil—something you contract out to a third party, check off your to-do list, and forget about shortly thereafter? Or is your mobile app a vital and integrated component of your marketing program? If you're like most organizations, you probably fall into the former category. It's no wonder, then, that app analytics and marketing platform Localytics reports that 20 percent of apps are used only once—and about 60 percent opened less than 10 times.

With mobile engagement on the rise, and technological advances enabling businesses to integrate apps deeper into their overall marketing strategy than ever before, it's time restart the conversation about mobile apps. Specifically, how can you move your app to a 2.0 version that delivers continued value to your customers and provides a superior mobile (and overall) experience?

Take one of my favorite apps: digital music service Spotify. This app keeps me engaged and coming back for more by allowing me to discover new artists and download specific albums or tracks for offline listening during my frequent travels. In addition, in-app inbox messages notify me what friends are listening to, exposing me to more great new music.

The awesome experience continues onto the desktop app, which syncs my preferences seamlessly between devices. And of course Spotify takes all this data and uses a really smart recommendation algorithm to highlight more music suggestions in its emails, which I almost always open because they're so relevant.

If you're still on the fence about whether moving your mobile app functionality beyond "find the nearest store location" is worth your time and resources, consider these three benefits:

1. Gain a new data source: What actions are contacts taking in your mobile app? Where are your customers right now? And how often do they come to your store? Apps can be rich sources of data that—with the right integrations back into your dynamic marketing tools—can enhance your knowledge of individual customers.

2. Send push notifications: According to the business intelligence firm Aberdeen Group, using mobile touch points—such as personalized push notifications—can increase conversion rates by 8.5 percent. Used strategically, these notifications can help you deliver timely, relevant information or offers linked to a customer's location and behaviors.

3. Access to a new inbox: The mobile app inbox delivers an all-new destination for marketers to reach—one that sports a new set of benefits (as in the Spotify example mentioned earlier). Beyond the fact that permission for sending is typically contained in your terms and conditions of usage (and doesn't provide a traditional email-like opt-out function), in-app inboxes allow marketers to send time-constrained offers and single-use promotional codes to specific users

in a true one-to-one manner. Yet because permission is different, marketers need to show restraint in using this new channel.

Taking the time to build and update apps to offer content and value that entices customers to download and repeatedly interact with them—as well as accept push notifications—allows marketers to tap into a whole new way of more strongly engaging their customers.

By taking steps to improve your in-app experience—and making these improvements a key objective for your marketing team—you'll be on the path to better understanding the behaviors that are manifesting themselves in the mobile app world and using this knowledge to create a more seamless, rewarding customer experience.

9 Data Capture and Hygiene

You're Only as Good as Your Database

When it comes to driving epic success with behavioral marketing, there's one element that's the best predictor of all: a focus on data. Although I believe in the Art of Marketing, data needs to be the fundamental basis of how we operate. That doesn't mean we deliver less-than-compelling content or ignore the human factors involved with great marketing. It does mean that we apply science first, then art—but more on that in a minute.

I've seen average marketers up their response rates by 50–100 percent by factoring for simple demographic elements such as age or gender or location. Demonstrating even the smallest bit of data-driven personalization can push response rates through the roof. From a behavioral perspective, some of my most progressive customers have an amazingly simple tactic: they resend a second version of every standalone email (same **exact** content, different subject line) to those who didn't open the first email two days after the initial send. Most often, this picks up another six to eight percent opens, and inevitably turns a conversion or two.

So let's dive deeply into the complex topic of data capture and hygiene. The most logical way to tackle the idea is from the top. I'll begin by describing how to think about the concept pre-implementation; then we'll talk through five key tactics that are the building blocks of great data focus, and finish up with how to make sure great isn't the enemy of good in your marketing effort.

Science versus Art

Many times, the data discussion starts and ends with a classically trained businessperson who's ended up in a marketing role. Although it's an overgeneralization to say all marketers begin from a place of less data than more data, it's absolutely true that marketers are not commonly bred from IT and business analyst types (who generally think numbers first). This means that the average marketer who's newly in charge of a decent-sized budget, a couple of staff, and some vague pressure to deliver revenue probably is not likely to rebuild the entire effort around data—even though that's almost always the most profitable way forward.

In some cases, the marketer has a direct background in—or has been significantly influenced by—the pure creatives on their team. It's easy to test different colored buy buttons in email creative and pick a winner to drive 3.6 percent more conversions; but it's much harder to rethink who you're targeting and when. This is the crux of whether you're a data-driven marketer. For those who think data first, the initial question is one of segmentation (who's getting this message?) versus one of creative execution (what's the call to action in the message?).

So although the science and art of marketing can absolutely co-exist in harmony, there is a very clear order to how we queue these two up. Any marketer today can instantly become more effective and behavioral-driven by improving their thinking around audience selection. The beauty of applying science (segmentation) before art (message) is that you'll almost always reduce the size of your audience, but almost always increase the relevance and revenue driven from each campaign.

In fact, I have at least five customers that drive in excess of 40 percent of their email-based revenue from less than 5 percent of their email volume. One scenario involved an ecommerce retailer who was having massive deliverability problems that caused them to hack off the least interactive 80 percent of their database (those who hadn't opened or clicked in the previous three months). And guess the outcome; yes, their revenue *increased*. How is this possible? Because the 80/20 rule is probably even too conservative in its theory that 80 percent of your revenue is driven by 20 percent of your customers.

For more market-side evidence, look at Amazon Prime members' spend versus non-Prime members. They've stated publicly that an average Prime member spends just over $1,500 annually, which is more than double the amount of non-Prime members at $693 annually. And don't forget the Prime members *pay* $100 for the privilege of doubling their spending.

At the end of the day, marketers need to think in terms of being significant catalysts for change—not just order takers. We need to own this transformation on behalf of our companies. Many days, we'll be able to directly measure our results in terms of increased sales or rising lead scores; but we need to have the courage to undertake this journey for a much larger reason. The relationship between your company and your prospect or customer must be based on two core elements: relevance and trust. And, yes, relevance depends on the science of marketing, and trust is driven by the art of marketing.

Why You? Why Now?

If we can become more data driven, chances are we'll also become much, much more effective at our jobs. So if this is such a great idea, then why isn't every company doing it? The simple reasons are effort and inertia. It's basic human nature to continue doing what we did yesterday, particularly if we've just taken a new role or if we're unsure about how to proceed. And yes, change is hard; but it's always easier when you're *leading* the change versus having to figure out how to adapt to it.

Let's look at a few common reasons why *you* bringing this mentality to your marketing programs is the right thing to do:

1. **Revenue cures all ills:** Although change of any kind can be hard to institute, the magic bullet that makes it all better is revenue. If I could give a single piece of career advice to any 25-year-old marketer today, it would be to drive more revenue based on the data you have at hand. You're going to have to prove yourself in your career, and now's the perfect time to start on a path few others will take because of the increased effort it requires.

2. **No one expects you to:** One of the coolest things about bringing these concepts to your role is that no one **ever** expects marketers to add business value. Our colleagues often see us as a shared service to the company, but the reality is we have massive amounts of customer data at our disposal. Knowing each campaign's response rate or seeing how web visitors get hung up in specific ecommerce flows are key insights we can turn into solid recommendations back to our business partners. Relish in the fact you're underestimated—and prove everyone else wrong.

3. **It begins with elements you control:** Don't think about trying to change the entire company's data approach right out of the gate. Find four to five ways you can make your world more data driven and show immediate lift. If you're an email marketing manager, use open data to segment users into active and nonactive users and then experiment with follow-up mailings to the most active openers. Once you prove lift in your world, then use that to gain permission to tackle bigger, company-wide efforts.

4. **Because no one else has:** Unfortunately, it is too often the case that everyone is utterly content to do it like we always have. If you hear this phrase at your company, consider it your single biggest career

opportunity and get down to business. If you're new to a job where this dynamic exists, go directly to the top of the organization with a rational, informed plan to lift revenue by being more data focused. Once you get their approval, just begin executing. You'll likely have lots of flack to deal with along the journey, but as long as revenue is going up, you're golden.

5. **Executives love sales:** It's worth saying out loud that this approach will absolutely get you promoted faster and more often. Increasing sales or spiking customer satisfaction is a sure way to bring kudos to you and your entire management chain—especially if you've pulled it off in a creative or resource-constrained way. It's up to you how you leverage these wins, but I know plenty of brilliant marketers who are content to make their boss, their boss's boss, and their colleagues in other departments the stars. I've always operated from a place of empowering my peers while clearly merchandising my effort to the smallest group of executives who guide my earning and promotion potential. This is an epic moment to be a team player, and if you're that personality type, you'll earn the undying trust of your peers—and they'll do amazing things for you down the road.

Data at the Speed of Business

For as long as I've been in tech (since the early '90s if you're keeping track), there's been a mantra to be more data driven. I remember in the late 1990s days of spending more than $800,000 on a booth at the world's largest technology tradeshow (Fall COMDEX in Las Vegas) to bring in Team Rollerblade. Imagine a 40-foot-high half-pipe in the Sands Convention Center with music blasting and elite athletes flying 60 feet above the floor. Amazing to watch? Yes. Related at all to our software business that targeted designers and illustrators? Not really. Was it data driven enough to at least capture booth leads based on the pure excitement of the show? Definitely not.

Certainly we've all run programs and campaigns we couldn't prove worked well. And we don't always have the luxury of making every element trackable and quantifiable. But that doesn't mean we shouldn't try. Being data driven is a journey. We're not going to get it right all the time, but every small improvement moves us closer to our destination.

This is why I always caution marketers to tackle data issues at the speed of business and to pick your battles carefully. Can you take a new role in the company, and immediately force changes in data policy? Maybe if you're the new chief marketing officer, but probably not.

You also need to stage up these changes over time for the simple reason of organizational continuity. Even if you could wave a magic wand and transform everything, it'd still take months to train and reorient your colleagues around a more data-driven approach. In fact, many groups beyond marketing will likely be your biggest challenges. If you've not been through the full budgeting and spend approval processes with a true finance department, you might not have seen how slowly the wheels of progress can move—but let me assure you that rapid change is not their specialty.

So although you need to be steadfast in your progress, you can't simply ignore the challenges associated with significantly changing a company's way of business. Becoming more data driven is not a one-time, week-long choice. It's a years-long journey that will have its wins and losses along the way. Set a strong pace that's comfortable in the benefits it achieves even if some of the old guard aren't as comfortable with the machinations along the way.

Hygiene or Capture First?

The final think topic we'll address before diving into tactics is how to effectively index your effort for capture and/or hygiene. It's difficult to do both initially and simultaneously, so you'll be more successful if you pick one to focus on first.

This decision is best made by looking critically at your current data set. If you're a mature marketing company with a CRM system already installed and thousands of customers and prospects in the buying cycle, then hygiene is probably your best first move. The reality is you already have 8 to 10 key data points on much of your customer set, and the most important question is whether that data is improving your closing ratio or not. Many times, key groups like inside sales or marketing ignore these additional data points because they're unsure of the data's reliability.

In this case, maintain whatever current data collection strategies you have in place but turn your eye toward more layers of validation. This might take the form of scrubbing your data against external sources to confirm you have companies classified in the correct standard industrial classification (SIC) codes to ensure the correct inside sales group is calling on the correct accounts.

It might also take the form of marketing-driven activities such as producing whitepapers on key customer topics, and then asking for specific additional data points from known users in the database. Confirming that you know exactly who the buyers and influencers are within your top 20 key accounts is a powerful place to work from. Regardless of how you get there tactically, your goal should be to make the data so bulletproof and insightful that the organization couldn't imagine not having it on hand to power smarter customer interactions.

If you're a new startup just building your prospect list or a company that drives most of your leads through paid media and other outbound strategies, then your weakness is much more likely to be depth of knowledge on your customer. I work with many marketers who only know the AdWords click source or referring URL for every prospect that lands on their site. They might actually have to engineer an entire sales process without ever even knowing their customers' email addresses.

If this sounds like your business, your job is to increase your depth of knowledge. The whitepaper registration tactic mentioned earlier works just as well here, so I always suggest this process start with a fully fleshed-out content strategy. We'll expand on content later in the book, but suffice to say you've got to build a solid exchange value that informs your prospect beyond your solutions and gets you deeper insight into your prospects' buying process.

One of the most important steps in driving deeper understanding of brand new prospects is to implement visitor tracking on your website. Any solid marketing automation platform like Silverpop has this capability immediately available, and it can assign unique identifiers to both known and anonymous users across your marketing spectrum. Once you've tagged the identity, you can begin associating multiple behaviors with that specific contact—ranging from follow-on site visits to registration events to email opens.

Using your site to begin tracking anonymous users and developing specific marketing programs to drive registration provide the foundation for building a much deeper knowledge set on your prospects. This is compelling for many reasons, but don't underestimate the power of understanding the lead source of a profitable customer. Knowing that your $6 cost per thousand (CPM) LinkedIn paid media effort is driving customers worth eight times as much annual revenue as your $3 CPM AdWords campaigns is the type of knowledge that will transform how you deploy your acquisition budgets.

It's also critical to think through how you expand your customer-level data through additional capture and appending. At Silverpop, we offer a feature called progressive forms that allows our clients to add up to hundreds of customer data points they'd like to capture from a specific prospect. Each time customers download a whitepaper or talk to a support rep, they're prompted to answer the next two to three questions in the queue; and it's completely personalized to the individual based on the sum total of what you know about them. After 60 to 90 days of this program running, marketers have a much deeper picture of a contact and have achieved that insight without throwing out a

15-field form that a buyer is sure to abandon (or fill with junk data) before completion.

From an external data sense, there are literally thousands of options and many ways to accomplish deeper insights. Some approaches will require your IT colleagues to add API (application program interface) calls to specific services that match your data up with external sources from credit reporting bureaus or other big data sources. If that's beyond your grasp, software-as-a-service options like InsideView allow a user to upload a spreadsheet of contacts to the system that returns an enhanced view driven by editorial, crowd-sourced, social, and webcrawled data. In fact, consulting firm Sirius Decisions summarizes the thinking this way: "Strong data organizations realize a 66 percent revenue advantage over those in the average category."

Five Key Tactics

Now that we've set our thinking straight on becoming more data driven, let's look at five foundational tactics for doing so. Again, there are hundreds of ways to arrive at the same level of improvement, and most of them are greatly dependent on your current status. Therefore, there's not one single path to enlightenment, metaphorically speaking. You can only make sure that you're covering the core functions, and place yourself on a long, steady journey of improvement.

Following are the big five items you need a definite plan to address. You don't have to be brilliant at each one before beginning deployment, but you do need a basic framework of a plan, and you need to be prepared to iterate quickly while in execution mode.

Master Database

First, a centralized master database is a prerequisite to being truly data driven. You can't analyze what you can't capture and store. That's not to say you have to go spend $5–7M on a giant on-premises database solution that's going to take epic amounts of IT involvement and spend. If you're starting from the absolute ground-up, don't consider anything other than this decade's class of very strong SaaS options.

Choosing which vendor works best with your company's specific situation is an art by itself. You can determine much of it by asking two key questions: "How big is our list?" and "How far outside of marketing do we need to work?" For most scenarios, the more marketing specific your database is, the more successful you'll be. It simply comes down to who sets the priorities, and you, of course, want that person to be *you*.

If you're held hostage by bigger forces—IT resources, 18-month enhancement cycles, and so forth—progress will be painfully slow, and you'll be forced to march to someone else's drum. The best possible scenario is to get your own marketing-only system and figure out how to integrate key data points from across your organization. And again, I'd almost exclusively recommend a cloud-based SaaS system that fits your company size and budget so you can benefit from a steady stream of new features (without having to endure in-house upgrade cycles) and reliable uptimes. Don't be fooled for one second by the lower entry costs associated with huge on-premises systems. Implementation, enhancements, and maintenance will ensure you spend more time and money than if you picked a new SaaS platform every three years.

Last, remember your database only needs to be as centralized as you can get it. If it's only marketing data but you sell via a direct sales force, then chart a course to integrate with the CRM system they have chosen. And if that's already decided, then ensuring your marketing database plays well with the CRM should be a key buying factor. Don't be satisfied with simple talking points from vendors on the integrations; make sure you see live demos of data flowing between the systems. Ask deeper questions around conflict resolution of conflicting data and how often the systems sync. On the other hand, I see some very shrewd marketers who license an SaaS tool and are able to migrate that into the key system of record for the company to build on.

Customer ID Scheme

Second, but also directly related to the master database, is the necessity to have a single ID view of the customer. The system of record that assigns and tracks that unique value—usually in the form of a 32-bit alphanumeric string—is what will begin the process of identifying your customers on a truly individual basis. Many days, your marketing automation platform is the right system of record, but on other days it could include your billing system if customer number is the unique ID. Alternatively, if you're a CRM-based shop, then that ID is likely the best choice assuming it bi-directionally integrates with your marketing automation system. This allows 360-degree reporting of customer interactions, and enables your organization to build solid path-to-close models that management can plan and staff around. This degree of insight into the buying process—and the quantification of marketing's role—is a reason to love this approach.

The other critical channel to consider is your website, which could tip the argument in favor of your marketing automation system as the primary platform in charge of identifying users. This is crucial because the normal buying cycle now heavily involves learning and communication via the web. Yet we know virtually nothing about these users even as they form their most long-lasting impressions of our products and company.

If you take this approach, you must ensure that your customer ID plan includes both anonymous and registered users. Most will be anonymous to start, and ignoring that huge segment won't work over time. As a best practice, your platform should drop cookies on anonymous visitors and retain their site behavior for at least 5 to 10 days while they're in research mode.

If, during the course of their visits, you deliver content or an offer that triggers a sign-up, you'll want all that anonymous site data drawn forward into their record. For example, knowing that your most technical whitepaper often leads to initial opt-in should give you a clear sense that educating your customer is Job One. This gives you a great sense of key site paths, and can strongly contribute to the customer journey mapping efforts we discussed in Chapter 7. It also helps you understand which offers and/or content creates the most compelling value proposition. Take this knowledge and sharpen your marketing tools to drive this golden moment even earlier in the cycle.

Basic Segmentation Rules

Once you think in terms of more data, you very quickly understand it requires that you understand segmentation and targeting at a deeper level—the third tactic needed. When you sent the same content to everyone, there was never a question of what advanced criteria you'd consider to cut the list down; you just blasted away to anyone who had an email address. This expanded data will now allow you to segment down to smaller audiences and deliver even more relevant and timely content.

As an example, think about how travel companies tier their loyal customers into high-level groups. In the Hilton Honors world, those levels are Blue, Silver, Gold, and Diamond. That top-level segmentation allows them to think broadly about benefits for each customer group— and to roll out specific products designed specifically for each segment. For instance, in-room Wi-Fi is free for Gold and Diamond members, so they can always refer to that benefit as part of any message to those segments.

I specifically call these 'basic segmentation rules' for a very important reason—they will absolutely change as your skills grow and your programs improve. You really only need to be familiar with the thinking and rough implementation of five to seven segments across your customer base. If you haven't considered segments at all, take a top-line crack at them before going much further in your data journey. If you're further along—say with a relatively deep set of persona models—you've got a great base.

Most often, your personas will be very personality and customer driven but might not have key individual metrics like lifetime spending. This is where your top-level segments will be overlaid with these newly developing customer views. So instead of marketing your clothing line directly to just your fashion-aware mom persona (female, 22 to 45, at least one child, etc.), you can now begin to overlay customer lifetime value (CLV) into the equation.

For example, if you've just launched your most expensive winter coat in the history of your clothing line, you could begin by marketing it only to customers who have spent at least $800 across at least two purchases in the last 12 months. Overlaying behavior-driven segments with your personas is a recipe for nice sales lifts in almost any ecommerce setting.

So think about your current segmentation rules, and then look for newly developing segments based on your new data points. Slicing the audience differently can be an enlightening moment for marketing— and stacking them together can really drive revenue.

Program Automation Capability

Once you've mastered segmentation thinking, the next logical question is: "How am I supposed to deal with all these little subgroups when I could barely keep up with my main list?" The answer is simply that your marketing will become more automated (tactic four), and, if done effectively, it will become much more relevant as well.

Let's use a common example you have likely seen in your inbox if you're an online shopper. The cart abandon email has risen in importance over the last two years to become a standard tactic for ecommerce marketers, and it's a perfect example of a behavior-driven, automated program.

It works likes this: a known user is browsing the site and places a specific SKU(s) in their cart but fails to complete the purchase process. This behavior is very strongly correlated to buying, but we can't be sure why the buyer did not convert. Maybe it was a change of mind when they saw the shipping charges; maybe the cat unplugged the computer. There's no way to truly know, so we set up an automated program to reach back out via email.

Some common best practices include sending the message ASAP after the abandon event (within the hour is ideal), and then following the message with at least one more. An ideal program would have an initial email almost immediately with a gentle reminder to buy; the second message a day later would outline specific reasons why it's the right shop to buy from; and a final message three days later might feature a discount offer to try and incentivize the conversion.

But clearly we can't manage this individually for every customer who abandons a cart. We execute this campaign via the automation functionality, and all we have to do is set up the front-end rules to determine who receives the messages—for instance, you might suppress someone from receiving more than one in a 45-day period even if they meet all the other criteria—and then deliver the template containing a mix of standard content and specific item and offer information. We truly don't care if a hundred or a million people go through the process each day; it's 100 percent automated. Those who spend time crafting the best content normally see at least a 20 percent conversion rate, and I've seen that number spike as high as 45 percent when it includes a very compelling offer.

The same thinking can work for almost any other phase in the buying cycle. Any time a desired group takes a specific action, you can reach out in a fully automated, highly scalable way to directly support the buying process. The automation function is what brings the segmentation work to life and drives home the revenue opportunity.

Dedicated Staff

You will notice how many times I refer to smart people making important decisions during my descriptions of all the preceding topics. This is the crux of great data-driven marketing. Not only do you need a plan to capture and clean your data; you also need dedicated people resources to really run this effort well. This is the fifth and final key tactic.

I know that getting a new headcount is probably one of the most difficult challenges marketers have, but it's critical to have someone specifically tasked with migrating your approach from mass marketing to data driven. I'm not saying that it can't be you, the mass marketer, at first, but someone who thinks like a database analyst can sure be of *huge* help in the process. Understanding everything from migrating data in automated ways to understanding when a behavior is statistically relevant is a skill you may not have yet developed.

The good news is that the new hire doesn't always have to come from the outside. I know many marketers who cultivate great internal relationships with the specific intent of grooming up someone from IT to come join marketing later this year. It's a smart strategy for a couple of reasons. Firstly, it gets the skill set directly integrated with your team, *plus* you're getting someone who understands the organizational-specific aspects of how to get things done quickly.

In fact, the last time I worked internally as a marketing director, I had two to three key personnel in IT that I went far out of my way to help. I even hired an email marketing manager with a specifically technical background, and sent her off to technical college to finish her degree on the company's dime. Having that level of technical ability close to my marketing thinking was such a powerful combination that

I brought her along with me as I moved out into the digital agency space as well.

So regardless of where you find someone (or even if you're the data geek), it only matters that there's someone dedicated to thinking through the data aspects of great marketing. Most often this means segmentation, data collection, and integrations but just as commonly can cross into program strategies. Find someone who straddles the worlds of IT and marketing, and you'll have a serious ace in the hole.

Conclusion

Although moving to a more data-driven marketing approach isn't easy, its benefits are clear. By segmenting our audiences into smaller and smaller buckets, we earn the opportunity to deliver smarter and smarter messages. And those smart messages convert at two or three or four times our normal one-to-many messages. Yes, it means more work, but there's a sizeable prize in the form of more revenue.

You can deliver on this data approach even if you control only the smallest slice of marketing data. Do the absolute best with the data you have, and find a solution that allows you to factor in more data over time as your organization sees the benefit. Maybe you'll only start with a simple welcome program that breeds loyal customers, but eventually your revenue success will convince your organization to integrate ecommerce purchase data into your system; then you'll see exactly what success looks like.

As I often say to our customers, **don't let great be the enemy of good**. Pick a starting point based on your current systems and skills, and chart a course for the next three to four quarters. Don't worry about making each iteration perfect. Any degree of data-driven insights you can plug into the process will help you drive better content and better results, so get started this week!

10 Campaign Creation

Segments, Logic, and Automation Are Your Friends, and Great Creative Matters More Than Ever

N ow that we've covered much of the prework required to be a great behavioral marketer, let's focus on executing within our actual campaigns. Granted, many marketers concentrate *only* on this stage today, but obviously I think success requires a much more holistic approach. Beginning from a more advanced starting point can only improve our end results.

I'll use another story from the extensive time I spend with our customers. I've worked with an ecommerce retailer who very clearly understands behavioral marketing, and continues to push its efforts forward. Like any great online seller, this retailer has become very effective at brilliant upfront welcome programs and really compelling cart abandon email series.

Its next level of automation is what the market calls browse abandon emails. This allows them to leverage website visit data to drive triggered email content after a contact visits a specific section. As a test, the retailer built a one-time email that was automatically sent to anyone who visited its website's "for him" section that featured a very simple headline

(Man, Oh Man), three best-selling products from that category, and a straightforward call to action to come back and shop.

That triggered email drives online conversion at almost 140 percent of the retailer's standard one-to-many messages (2.2 percent versus 1.6 percent), and was so successful that it went back and built out similar campaigns for each of its other seven site sections. The important thing to remember about these fully automated campaigns is that they truly are a one-time effort, and are the epitome of set-and-forget. (That doesn't mean do go back and refresh your content every 60 to 90 days.) There might be 1,000 people a day who meet the criteria, or there might be 10,000. Either way, it capitalizes on a lost buying moment and drives interested customers back to the site to convert.

Segments Matter

We've talked a bit about segments previously, but I want to clearly underscore that segmentation should be your first view of any campaign effort. Thinking more deeply about who receives your communications can remake your entire approach.

For example, what if your business owners were only prepared to deliver a 15 percent discount to your entire customer base as a purchase incentive for fear of giving away too much top-line revenue? Yet you could show them a small subset of the audience that were high-value customers with significant spending patterns that would spend three times more this quarter if you offered a one-time 25 percent off coupon. Having the data and customer insight built into your segment models to deliver this kind of insight is where the most effective marketers are headed.

So let's talk about a few layers of segmentation you might begin with and a few you can build toward. Although you could slice and dice your customer base almost any way one could imagine, there are three primary ways to think about segmentation: demographic, behavioral, and fully scored. Although scoring is really a superset of demographic and behavioral, I'm going to take the three separately because there's a lot of art to great scoring models.

Demographic data is a great place to begin your segmentation thinking. Normally we can run a quick snapshot report to understand how our customer base is split by gender, family size, location, or email domain. These very interesting splits can be the basis for some solid content-sharpening exercises.

For example, understanding that your primary multipurchase buyer is most often a female with at least one child can help guide both the content and the offers you make via email. You might aggressively experiment with images that include families or offer replenishment-based ordering designed for busy moms. The details of how and what you test will obviously be specific to your business, but you see the point: isolate a specific demographic element, and then market based on that buyer's wants and needs.

This approach also allows you to send custom messages to specific domains in the event of any new ISP changes that might significantly affect your marketing effort to a certain set of customers. Yes, I'm referring to the Gmail users in your database. The never-ending march of enhancements within Gmail make it almost a certainty that you'll want to communicate exactly how your recipients should manage the next feature that impacts how, when, and where they receive your messages within Gmail. This practical take on segmentation allows us to improve our marketing game just as much as communicating effectively to moms.

Let's pause before we talk about behavioral segmentation to discuss the difference between implicit and explicit preferences as it directly relates to your demographic segmentation strategy. Explicit preferences are what your customer will tell you via a form or an interaction with sales. For example, when someone opts into your mailing list, they might self-report as a woman; clearly we'd have no reason to doubt their selection. Yet interestingly, there's an implicit application of gender that could prove to be a very valuable insight in creating your dynamic marketing programs.

I have one UK-based retailer who actively looks at explicit versus implicit preferences when deciding what items to highlight in its marketing emails. Even though Jane Smith might have indicated she was female on sign-up, if she continually views men's items—perhaps in an attempt to improve the wardrobe of a potentially disinterested significant other—then the retailer will migrate the content accordingly. Its results show a small lift in conversions, but this is more about subtly demonstrating to your customers that your marketing is paying attention at an individual level.

This type of implicit segmentation also puts us on the path to understanding how recipient behaviors are often the most powerful elements on which to track and act. The retailer in the preceding example looked very specifically at website page-view data—an excellent way to begin thinking about behavioral segmentation. It's the epitome of the old adage "Believe what I do, not what I say."

Although the cart abandon and browse abandon emails we discussed at the beginning of this chapter are great for ecommerce retailers, there's an equivalent behavior-driven aspect to almost every industry segment and persona. For the B2B marketer, understanding the velocity of visits from multiple people in a single organization over a week or a month might be a significant indication that you're in the final consideration set for a request for proposal (RFP) or your outright selection. And maybe the outcome of capturing that behavior is twofold: a subtle, benefit-oriented email to the primary buying contact and a CRM call flag sent to an inside sales rep to reach out in person.

This focus on tightly segmenting your audience based on their actions is the underlying principle of behavioral marketing as a whole. Considering the full scope of what someone says, does, and buys can give a marketer critical insight, not just into that individual but also into others who might act and buy similarly.

And finally, let's dive into the topic of scoring and how that can overlay and deeply inform your segmentation strategies. Traditionally, the idea of scoring behaviors was a B2B tactic designed to bring some sanity to a long and winding buying cycle that might include multiple channels and dozens of interactions. The primary thinking is to score each key event with an appropriate number of points so we can build a long-term view of the process.

The number of points awarded might look something like the examples shown in Figures 10.1 and 10.2, from one of our customers. You'll notice they've outlined scoring modifications on three key points: demographic, behavioral, and time. Although each is appropriately weighted based on how important it is to the end conversion, it's critical to recognize the entire process is also factored for time. This is because they clearly understood that if someone shows interest early but hasn't purchased in the first 90 days, then that individual almost never does, hence the –5000 points that are applied on the 91st day. This, in effect,

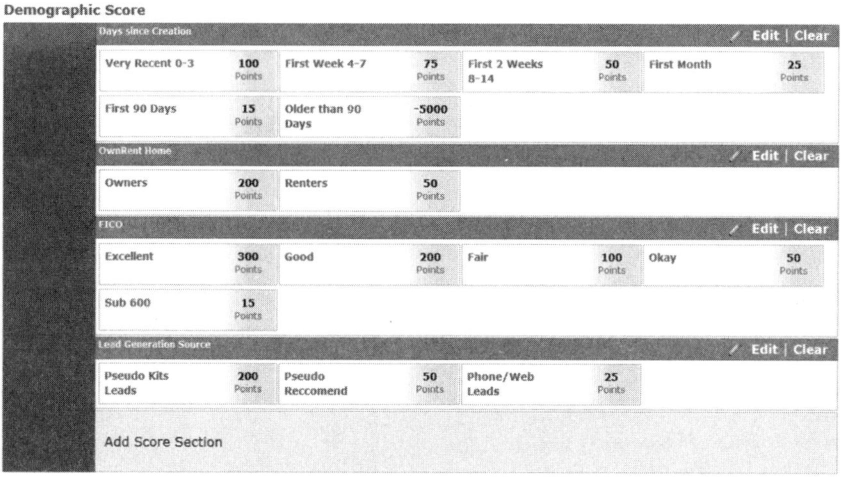

Figure 10.1 Demographic Score

Behavioral Score

			Edit | Delete
Activity	Clicked Buy Now in Drip		
	Clicked Buy Now in Drip ∞	200 Points	
	Clicked Other Links in Drip		Edit | Delete
	Clicked Other Links ∞	100 Points	
	Opened an Email		Edit | Delete
	Opened an Email ∞	15 Points	
	Visited lifeshield.com		Edit | Delete
	Visited .com ∞	50 Points	
	Visited /buynow		Edit | Delete
	Visited the pseduo site ∞	100 Points	

Figure 10.2 Behavioral Score

removes that contact from the majority of their marketing programs almost instantly.

So each prospect at any moment during the sales cycle has a specific score, and all scores are ranked comparatively in groups as shown in Figure 10.3.

There's now an absolutely objective, numerical view of where every prospect is within the buying cycle. The final step in their analysis was

Ranking

					Edit | Clear
A+	is greater than or =	2000 Points			
A	is between	1500 Points	and	1999 Points	
B+	is between	1000 Points	and	1499 Points	
B	is between	750 Points	and	999 Points	
B-	is between	500 Points	and	749 Points	
C	is between	250 Points	and	499 Points	
D	is between	100 Points	and	249 Points	
F	is less than or =	99 Points			

Figure 10.3 Ranking of Prospects within the Buying Cycle

Overall Score	Conversion
>2000	60.00%
>1500	5.88%
>1000	9.52%
>750	11.63%
>500	8.46%
>250	4.25%
>0	1.20%
Behavioral Score	**Conversion**
>1000	20.83%
>750	9.62%
>500	9.92%
>250	5.84%
>0	2.63%

Figure 10.4 Deep analysis of the conversion data showed a strong correlation between overall scores and top-line conversion percentages, but when dissected even further the importance of customer behaviors were immediately apparent with conversions more than double the rate of the overall scores.

to map together the scores and ranks, then calculate six months of conversion behavior together as a baseline. Although they looked at both overall scores (demographic + behavior), you can see in Figures 10.4 and 10.5 that they found the strongest correlation between the behavioral score and true conversion.

Armed with this data, they realized that their most important job was to close more sales among the top two segments of engaged users— A's and B's. They felt confident that if they sharpened their content and involved inside sales at the exact moment someone rose above a 750 score, then they'd drive significantly more revenue. And they turned out to be exactly correct.

By deploying smarter closing tactics, they saw more than three times lift in the number of conversions among the top three segments of

Lead Rank	Conversion
A	9.85%
B	9.26%
C	1.82%
D	1.32%
F	2.22%

Figure 10.5 And by ranking the conversion rates, they created a banded lead rank that powered yet another view of how often specific audiences were moving to final conversion.

prospects. You'll also notice that they decided to split those top three segments into finer groups (see Figure 10.6, where A+, B+ and B− were added to the original A–F range) in order to drive even more specific offers and incentives at buyers close to conversion. For a company that had little idea where its prospects were in the overall buying process, this level of quantification had a major revenue impact on their business.

It's clear how concerted segmentation allows us to isolate and market to very specific customers on a one-to-one basis. When we invest time in understanding our customer's intent and where it lies in the overall process, we can roll out an entirely new set of tactics and messaging to support stronger conversion rates.

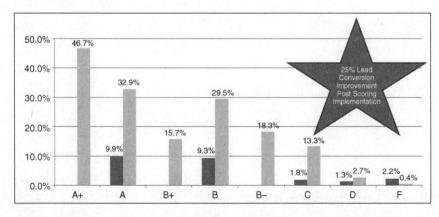

Figure 10.6 Conversion Results Across Two Versions of the Program

Logic, Queries, and Data, Oh My

Although this segmentation is obviously helpful, there's an underlying aspect of logic we should cover quickly in the context of campaign creation. It's one that manifests both during initial audience selection and at each step during an automated campaign.

We apply this logic in the Silverpop platform via a query engine. Before you get too scared about being a marketer in charge of queries (normally of the SQL [structured query language] variety, and the job of an IT person), the best SaaS platforms out there make this a very simple proposition. It's merely a matter of stacking up various demographic, behavioral, and scoring elements into a logic layer and deciding when it applies to the data.

For example, a query designed to build an initial segment might look something like Figure 10.7.

You can see the query factors for five separate layers here, which should, therefore, create a highly specific set of users. You'll notice across the top of the screenshot where you can add any other number of variables into the equation. So if you wanted a larger group to receive

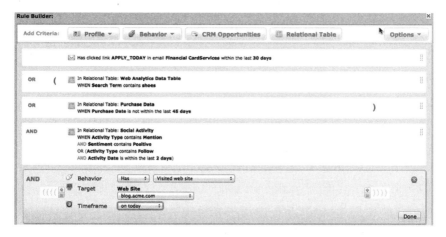

Figure 10.7 Query Designed to Build an Initial Segment

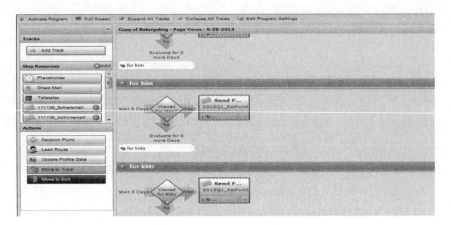

Figure 10.8 An Automated Browse Abandon Campaign

a specific communication, you might simply remove the social inter-action layer, which should have the effect of doubling or tripling the number of people who will receive this specific message.

This logic layer, therefore, creates the first cut of prospects to receive an automated mailing. Just as importantly, you can apply this same exact method to any decision point of an automated program. So the net effect is an increasingly relevant audience-selection method based on increased activity by the prospect. Our marketing is literally getting smarter as it engages more deeply with our cus-tomers—and we're architecting a constantly developing stream of content to support the exact moment in each buyer's individual journey.

Being able to layer this logic over real-time users flowing in and out of the buying process across all your channels becomes a very important new way to think about one-to-one marketing. Not only can a marketer pull ad hoc reports to see what specific audience counts look like by numbers of elements in a query; a marketer can also report on specific behaviors that are key junctions and how those relate to end conversion.

Automating for Epic Scale

By now you're probably trying to figure out how to put all these program enhancements into action. No marketer has a chance of using these tactics to scale up their efforts unless you have a serious automation engine. You simply can't—and shouldn't—ever try this in a manual way by scrubbing consecutive Excel spreadsheets and loading up a new list every time you send a campaign.

To truly move to a behavioral marketing view, you need an automation engine that brings to life all the data and segmentation work you've done to get to this point. And again, this is a time to choose a platform that can manage the amount of contacts you have in your lists today—and what you expect in the next 12 to 18 months—without sweat.

Although all these rules and logic are easy for a marketer to build, the horsepower required to keep them running smoothly isn't inconsequential. If you want to score a behavior such as email opens and you have a database of 20 million, make sure to review your vendor's capability to handle 3–4 million scoring events in the course of 10 to 15 minutes following a full-list send. Don't find yourself in the unenviable position of asking a B2B tool designed for lists of 50,000 people to do the volume of work required for a list of 50 million users.

The other great benefit of automating your marketing effort is that you can simply do more with the same number of people. We have a customer who manages an absolutely huge marketing effort covering nine products, a Silverpop database of over 100 million, a bi-directionally synched Salesforce database of over 15 million and in excess of 500 million emails sent annually with a full-time staff of three—yes only *three*—people. Clearly they're very experienced and have very complicated cross-sell and up-sell campaigns across all those various products, but they've slowly created an epic set of automated programs over the last 18 to 24 months, and they pay strong dividends in revenue growth.

Great Creative Matters More Than Ever

It's easy and tempting to get caught up in all this new thinking around behavioral marketing. However, it's also important to remember that this new approach means that your creative execution matters more than even now. Are you willing to go to all this work in audience selection and data hygiene to then deliver the same tired email newsletter every two weeks with 10 links? I certainly hope not!

If anything, you should be thinking about ways to 10 or 100 times your creative executions to these even more compelling customer moments. You should absolutely be thinking in terms of dynamic templates that have data-driven elements based on demographic or behavioral customer data.

Before we go much deeper into creative, let's talk about A/B and multivariate testing. There are lots of schools of thought on if, when, and how much you should be testing email content. A most practical approach should be defined by two primary elements: your current performance and how many people you have working on email.

If you're a solo practitioner supporting six business units and you don't know what day it is, then biting off true multivariate testing that could produce 36 or 64 versions of individual creative for a single campaign would be an absolute nightmare. If, on the other hand, you have a campaign that you think is underperforming but you can't quite sort out why, then diving into subject line and other spot testing makes great sense. Maybe look at specific calls to action, button colors, or using different images in your message.

Even though most platforms let you test on-the-fly using automated methods, one element not to mess around with is the send-from address. Your users come to expect communications from a specific email address and name; this is a key element when they're scanning their inboxes, considering which messages to consume and which to delete. Most marketers I know think the send-from address is among the first three decision points for any email's consideration—especially in the mobile channel, where most of us have open rates above 60 percent. So stick to testing the contents and subject line of the message, and don't bite off more than you can reasonably chew.

Beyond testing, the question of responsive design is one most marketers have fielded in the last 12 to 18 months. How your content renders on the major mobile devices is a critical question—but one that's fraught with asterisks, what-ifs, and fringe cases.

A simple example is the difference in how iOS and Android handle message width on a mobile device. iOS will display the message in auto-width mode, which in effect makes the content as wide as the widest graphic element regardless of how small the text becomes as a result. Conversely, Android pins the message to the top-left corner; if the message requires a side scroll to see beyond the available pixels, then that's how it works. Neither is right or wrong, but it clearly affects how you should design your content. Anchoring a call-to-action button in the right-hand column would not be smart for Android users. You also wouldn't want to reuse a 700-pixel-wide header graphic from your website in an email for iOS because the font would be reduced to something around 6 pixels, and will almost certainly require the recipient to pinch and zoom—and it's highly doubtful they even undertake that much effort.

These days I'm much more likely to recommend our customers apply some radical simplification to their campaigns as opposed to trying to factor for every one of the hundreds of screen sizes now between phones, tablets, and desktops. (And don't forget, true responsive design for email requires a separate HTML body for each width variation, so you're not going to want to shove 10+ versions into a 250k email—even in this age of broadband.) Beyond simplifying your effort, the benefits of clean, one to two product emails with clear calls to action extend all the way to recipient engagement.

Even in nurture programs, designing to optimize for the next step in the process is an absolute best practice. I recently saw an example at a European conference of a six-part mailing that only sent the next message to openers of the previous message. By the time the campaign was complete, just over 25 percent of the people were still following the storytelling effort, and the open rate on message six was an astounding 92 percent!

So although most of the examples I've used in this chapter focused on email, remember that designing great campaigns is a job we need to master in all channels. Often, this means leaning on colleagues across our organization, including key functions like customer support and outbound sales. You'll want to share your top-line messaging and existing digital-program details with your peers as they build out call scripts and offer matrixes to give to their reps. Making sure you inform these other customer-facing channels of any major promotions and/or data collection efforts underway is a great way to maintain solid working relationships across your company.

The bottom line is your prospects and customers are being bombarded by dozens or hundreds of other emailers every single day. Fighting for your share of attention requires an almost magical combination of audience segmentation, timely automation, and stunning creative. When you can discover the ideal combination of events that drive conversion for you, get to work automating it instantly—and continue to dial it in over time.

11 Behaviors and Mobile

Yes, It's Radically Different Than Every Other Channel

Although we've explored most channels and their requisite benefits, when revising your marketing approach to include behaviors, mobile requires some extra time. It's not just because the rise of mobile has been a tidal wave with the email marketing space over the last two years (which it absolutely has). It's also due to the fact that there are so many unique behavioral-driven aspects to this channel that are rewriting the top-line rules for how we communicate with our customers.

It might feel funny five years from now to have singled mobile out as a unique channel—because by then, that's where every interaction will be taking place, in the form of notifications on watches or windshields or on virtual reality (VR) headsets. Almost every marketer I know has been on a journey toward a more mobile user base since about 2010, and there's no end in sight. You'll have to continually determine how to refactor your entire communications strategy for faster conversations, smaller bits of information, and an always-on knowledge of a person's physical location. So let's not miss the opportunity to build this natively into our behavioral marketing effort from the beginning.

The History of Serious Mobile

Although you can debate what started the mobile-first revolution, almost everyone agrees the rise of the smartphone—both Apple and Android—was the gasoline on the fire. When we began to carry around serious computing power (like a Cray supercomputer's worth in an iPhone) in these small devices that also have GPS capabilities, some really cool things started happening.

Before that, mobile communication was about short message service (SMS)—and most people never even knew how that worked—at least, marketers certainly didn't in the early days. But the rise of the GPS chipset signaled a parallel rise of location-based startups around the 2005–2006 timeframe. Think early innovator Foursquare who rose from the first generation of location-based startups and continues to innovate its way into the directory and recommendations space.

One of the early user experience limitations for mobile was the same genius that led to its rise: that hot new GPS chip. The problem was that the chip required a ton of power to keep on all the time while waiting for the user to do something relevant like check-in or visit a specific store. Once the operating system makers sorted out the wrinkles there, location-powered events started to become mainstream data points for users and marketers alike.

As such, we have multiple tiers of GPS data today, users have the privacy controls to individually select which apps can or cannot track locations, and Apple's iOS 8 even has an always-on "Recent Places" list buried deep in the settings that some of the smartest app developers are leveraging for location-level data.

Now that location is as easy to track with a mobile app as virtually any other value about a user, of course marketers are beginning to factor for it in their queries and audience segmentation. It might play out like this in the marketing automation world:

Jen is an email marketing manager for a ski shop and is trying to drive cross-sell between her online store and her 10 retail locations. Not everyone who shops online is close enough to a physical location to be a candidate, so she's interested in location.

Her first indicator is simply known users with their addresses on file, who are easy to include in her standard queries to drive email messaging. However, there's a completely separate group of users who may not have a completed profile but who are walking down the street in front of (or across from) her 10 stores. By leveraging her mobile app's location capabilities and some basic geo-fencing programming, she's able to work with her agency to build an app-level notification program that triggers every time one of the app users walks by.

Jen may make the exact same offer she would to her email recipients (10 percent off or a free ski tune-up) or she may do something even more timely and compelling—like inviting people to stop in on a rainy day for hot chocolate. And, yes, pulling local weather information from an API (application program interface) in real time to change a normal message to the hot chocolate invitation is completely doable.

In fact, she might have an all-new cross-channel query that looks like this:

Anyone who's visited her site at least twice in the last six months

{AND}

Anyone who's spent at least $50 in the last 24 months online

{AND}

Anyone who's spent less than $20 in the last 24 months in-store

{AND}

Anyone who walks by the store

The result could be her best possible offer—20 percent off any one item in the store and free shipping for their next online purchase. This is exactly the kind of channel synchronicity most marketers would love to drive—and while executing it still requires some specialized players, all the pieces of the puzzle are widely deployed across the mobile spectrum.

And I haven't even included the most compelling location-based technology that's coming to market widely in the next two to three years in this user story: beacons. I don't want to devolve this into a technology for technology sake's discussion, so I'll just say that beacons will do the same thing for in-store location (imagine which aisle or which section) that the mobile phone did for map-level location. It's going to refine the meaningful distance down to two feet instead of 200 feet, which will make for yet another revolutionary moment for marketers.

Email versus SMS versus Apps

So now that we have anywhere between 2 and 20 communications methods baked into our smartphones, marketers must make a seriously momentous decision when it comes to behaviors: which communications lever do I pull when I track a behavior? You can make excellent arguments for all three options, so let's do a quick dive into each one's particular strengths:

1. **Email:** Regardless of how much people complain about being inundated by it, email is still an amazing channel to drive both sales (think cart abandon campaigns) and user re-engagement (think about the "We haven't seen you in awhile" message you get from your favorite online retailer). It has its challenges in the mobile world—particularly if you've ignored the fact most consumer brands now see more than 60 percent of their opens on mobile devices—but it's so pervasive that it works. Email's downside lies in our need to depend on external entities (Internet service providers) to deliver it to our customers. They play a gatekeeper role in that delivery because of an insane amount of bad actors generating SPAM in the trillions per day. It's also an opt-in based channel, so we can lose the ability to email a great lifetime customer based on a single screwup on our end that leads to them opting out.

2. **SMS:** Although it's always been a challenge for marketers to implement good SMS programs—or maybe *because* it's always been a challenge, so it hasn't risen to a commonplace practice—SMS has remained a bastion of interaction. Some marketers I know report 90 percent open rates on text messages. Its power lies in the combination of its simple but interruptive nature. I don't want to get too esoteric here, but you should think about SMS as the first-ever version of app notifications—with the phone being the app. If done well, I expect the app notifications we'll discuss next to enjoy an interaction quotient more like SMS (~80 percent opened) than email (~20 percent opened). SMS is also important because it's universal across almost all cell phones regardless of whether it's the latest Samsung Galaxy model or a Nokia 7200 from 2002.

3. **App notifications:** Finally, the newest communication channel within mobile is the app-level notification. Although there are currently some pretty serious constraints—for instance, you have to have a specific company's app downloaded to enable the function—I expect the use cases to get friendlier with the rise of connected devices like watches and other jewelry-oriented form factors. App notifications share the same interruptive nature of an SMS message, but also provide some really cool differentiators from traditional email. In addition to the pop-up notifications we normally think of, some app developers are moving to a world with in-app mailboxes. This mimics a typical email box, but with a few key differences: (1) it can also have a pop-up notification with the message; (2) there's no separate opt-in required and we don't have to gather some user-entered information to know where to send the message—although providing some user controls and outlining the rules of the app inbox in your terms and conditions are solid best practices; and (3) perhaps most important, you can expire a message in an app user's mailbox as easily as you sent it. Imagine the flexibility this provides to online sellers who have limited items for sale or someone who

wants to cap limit the number of coupon redemptions on a specific item based on a co-marketing deal with the manufacturer.

Just by looking at these three message types within mobile communications, you can see how complicated using them together could become. SMS has an almost universal application, but hard-core marketing is typically very carefully limited by each user—and typically is limited to two to three of their best friend brands (more on this concept in Chapter 15).

Where might this go over the next two to three years? Odds are that marketers will offer our customers the choice of where they want to be contacted—and about what topics. So they might pick newsletters for their email inbox, sale notifications by SMS, and discount offers by app notification. Or they may opt-out of SMS, or not download your app so there's no inbox to send to. Whatever ends up happening, giving the customer the choice will keep interaction and response rates more productive.

The Fragmentation of Communication Itself

If you want to imagine the real future state—and understand why you should be thinking radically about behavioral marketing and mobile technology right now—it seems that communication is in the process of being sharded into a million tiny pieces. And the end deliverable is *not* going to be an email newsletter with the same six stories that goes to everyone on your list. Every person will have his or her own interest graph that's powered by a combination of what they say and do.

I imagine that information will be chopped into such small pieces that we'll be able to drive incredible relevance in terms of when and who we deliver it to. Data points that car-buying services charge us money for today (average price paid for a Chevy Camaro in Omaha, Nebraska) are going to be a simple search you set up once and you get notified any time there's a change. You also get notified every time you enter an auto dealership—and if it's a factory-owned location, you also get the car's invoice pricing included. It won't be some clumsy attempt by a car manufacturer to send you a brochure; it'll be timely, dead-on relevant information delivered to you at the exact moment you need it by a semi-objective third party. (I'm also convinced that paid listings and sponsored content will be much harder to get rid of.)

You can ignore my future analysis or marketing and communications if it helps you sleep better at night, but you should keep your eye on one trend that will define exactly how fast my future world comes to fruition: wearable computing. Google Glass was an overly geeky first attempt at integrating content into a wearable device, and anyone thinking logically about human interaction probably could have predicted its demise. The next generation of watches and virtual reality headsets are much more likely to be the hardware behind this new revolution in communication.

Conclusion

Although mobile has likely been the biggest challenge for even the most traditional marketers over the last couple years, it's pretty clear things are only going to get harder. We'll look back and laugh at the days when the discussion around responsive design for HTML emails was the issue concerning everyone. That's because we'll be back to trying to refactor our most dynamic channel yet again based on a new use case or device.

In fact, mobile might actually be the ideal place for a marketer to take on behavioral marketing for two very clear reasons: (1) it's so hard you're probably going to outsource most of it, so why not include behaviors from the beginning? and (2) there's not going to be a single platform more likely to generate the types of behaviors you can absolutely bank on.

Someone opening an email or calling a call center is nice—and you can use that data to incrementally improve follow–up communications.

But knowing someone walked into a retailer and had looked at the same item on the website yesterday, and delivering a pop-up offer on the spot is a killer use case. If you think your desktop selling strategy was exploded by mobile only in terms of what device your messages were opened on, wait until you see your entire marketing effort deconstructed into tiny bits that are delivered in real time and convert at 50–60 percent. The next 10 years are going to be a wild ride as marketing goes native on mobile, and I'd suggest a minimally viable strategy is playing around the edges of the game while things are blowing up at an epic pace.

12 Measurement and Optimization

Creating a Framework and Moving Your Own Goalposts

Let's first clarify one major land mine. Any conversation on measurement and the email channel should begin at this critical point: open rates and click-through rates (CTR) are almost irrelevant numbers. Not only should they not be your default method of quantifying success; they're becoming even less relevant over the next 3 to 4 years. Although your problems will initially manifest in email open and click metrics, you won't be able to determine the source of the problem without further information. If the metaphorical canary dies, stop what you're doing and fix the bigger systemic problems you have.

Why do we start with this conversation around such a specific channel and generally accepted metric? For the simple reason that taking our thinking beyond our current approach also means we need to reengineer our metrics. We cannot measure how we execute in the future by how we did things in the past. If this is our default approach, then we're not pushing ourselves hard enough.

For example, let's say your baseline open rate is 22 percent, and your click-through rate (CTR) is 12 percent. Those would be solid numbers for most email marketing programs; but there are a ton of issues that can hide behind such high-level numbers. Ask yourself this slightly existential (but absolutely relevant) question: What about the other 78 percent? What are you missing in a value proposition to that large percentage of your audience? And are you looking at click-to-open rate (CTOR), which divides unique clicks by unique opens as another layer of detail into click data?

We can do much better in the measurement and optimization space, and we'll cover some very granular strategies in this chapter. Although the type of your business has some impact on how you measure (it'd be tough to have customer lifetime value as your primary metric if you're in the third-party lead generation business), there's a framework for how to think this through.

By looking at quantifying improvements in each channel, we can chart a course for an overhauled view of customer success. Some days it'll have nothing to do with revenue but will be much more customer-satisfaction focused. So keep those minds open, and let's dive in.

Mixing the Right Channels

In setting the right frame for this chapter, let's focus on the following list of channels for measurement and optimization—introducing each with why we care about them:

1. **Email:** As I've said before, email is absolutely the channel of conversion when done well. Additionally, it offers very strong automation capabilities. Very few users will opt-out, complain, or have negative feelings about email when we execute well. It's a generally accepted method of marketing almost worldwide.

2. **Direct mail:** Although more expensive and complex, direct mail absolutely has its role to play in both large-scale acquisition and ultra-targeted nurture programs. There's also been an interesting rebalancing of attention metrics over the years as fewer companies execute direct. In today's world, a well-placed mailer can be a really

good option to drive new-mover utility sign-up or a great way to add an incredibly relevant touch point in the middle of the long-term complex sale. Your message might be one of four in someone's physical mailbox, but one of 200 in their email inbox.

3. **SMS:** Mobile messaging in general is the most effective way to reach our customers—particularly when they're physically near your location or when they want small chunks of highly relevant information. And because SMS is a universal format that works across all carriers and devices, it enjoys astronomical engagement rates when done well. I'll say it again, I have customers who report SMS open rates of 90 percent!

4. **App notifications:** If SMS is the king of engagement, then app notifications should be the zenith of relevance. Many of the same location dynamics are in play and should definitely be driving your content strategy. Beyond the notification layer, there's a developing strategy around in-app inboxes that offer an entirely new email-like communication path that's devoid of all the legal and algorithmic pressures of sending simple mail transfer protocol (SMTP) email via an Internet service provider (ISP).

5. **Paid media:** The tight targeting capabilities of paid media represent the strongest pure acquisition strategy available to most marketers. The fact that we have fully automated the concepts of pricing and user targeting across almost every social network and many banner networks instantly provides smart marketers with a direct line to prospects. The compression of CPM rates, along with the rise in cost-per-click (CPC) and cost-per-acquisition (CPA), have made digital channels even more compelling from a cost perspective.

6. **Social:** Although we're still early on the topics of measurement and optimization in social media, it's a channel most marketers simply cannot ignore. The best news is you don't necessarily have to completely solve every resource allocation or voice-of-the-brand

issue for social to be relevant. Some of the smartest marketers use social as a listening platform first, then as a publishing platform. You need to stake your claim to user names on the platforms most relevant to your business, but think of it as a marathon as opposed to a sprint. Pace yourself, be smart, and act deliberately, but always remember it absolutely is a race—and, therefore, there are winners.

Five Deeper Views

Although every marketer will mix and match the preceding channels to their best use, this chapter isn't going to devolve into the age-old topics of digital versus traditional, earned versus paid media, or how to write a great direct marketing letter.

To truly move the needle in these more competitive and social-powered times, we need to measure and act more deeply. It's not enough to drive a few more percent of clicks on your email campaigns or 10 more coupon redemptions from your bulk mailer. By now, your individual channels should be relatively well optimized, and you should be thinking almost exclusively about how to combine them to orchestrate a better buying experience for your customers.

Toward that end, I'm going to outline five emerging metrics for you to consider when planning your marketing programs. You can think about these as individual attributes you're looking to isolate and market to, but you can also think of them as segments when applied across your entire prospect and customer audiences. Understanding the finest points of these customer journeys will allow you to ideally deploy all the channel tactics we described earlier in this book.

For example, let's say you've got a segment of potentially high-value customers who you have determined are deep considerers based on their actions (for this example, we'll define the term as someone who's visited your site at least three times in the last 30 days and has seen an in-person demo of your software product). In this case, orchestrating an outbound telesales call to gain that last mile of understanding—and to ask for the sale in person—is often a winning strategy.

You could look at each of these "segments" in a very quantified light as well. What percentage of your new leads in a given quarter become repeat purchasers within six months? How successful are you at cultivating deep considerers from new leads within the first year of nurture marketing? Begin tracking metrics like these on your KPI (key performance indicator) dashboard, and that process is very likely to generate some all-new insights.

So let's dive in and look at five emerging criteria that you can quantify and track over time:

1. Repeat purchasers
2. Deep considerers
3. Raving fans
4. Disinterested recipients
5. Percentage of completed records

Repeat Purchasers

Although focusing on this audience isn't necessarily new for the most advanced marketers, too many ignore repeat purchasers almost completely. As author Paul Farris contends in his book *Marketing Metrics: The Definitive Guide to Measuring Marketing Performance,* selling to an existing customer is 50 percent easier than to a brand new prospect. This point is proven based on what I see in working with hundreds of marketing groups.

So if you're running a successful ecommerce operation and you're not marketing separately to existing (and recent) customers, it's time to rethink your approach. In Chapter 7, Customer Journey Mapping, we discussed the path to first purchase as distinct from path to repeat purchase—for an important reason. Gaining enough mindshare to drive a transaction is not a minor victory; you've gotten the right message to the right buyers while they are in the buying mindset. And just as importantly, you now have data on those individuals. Did you have to offer an incentive? How many times have they purchased from you in the last 60 days? Are they buying commodity or highly specialized items? What's the expected repurchase cycle for the items they're buying?

The same is absolutely true if you're selling longer-lead, higher-dollar items—although you might logically have a deeper focus on driving postpurchase recommendations from satisfied customers. Or you might view the purchase decision as the beginning of a long-term product experience that you'd like your customer to share with your community.

For example, the purchase of a specific level of luxury or performance automobile like the BMW 5-series or a Nissan GTR could certainly be the turning point for the manufacturer's marketing efforts. The manufacturer could elegantly move from the feature-by-price-by-competition conversation to one much more focused on enjoying the vehicle—and creating a lifetime of stories and memories with it.

In this specific vertical, I'm always surprised how much of the ultra-passionate community and fandom takes place outside the confines of the original brand on sites like bimmerpost.com or benzworld.org. Although I'm not naïve enough to think we marketers could own this conversation, it seems too few of us are willing to invest the resources to have that deeper postpurchase conversation and to learn from our most vocal supporters, whether that's good or bad. If nothing else, consider how much future product and positioning insight could be gained from a built-in focus group.

Deep Considerers

Although this would seem to skew more toward B2B based on the length of selling time, you can absolutely think about this in terms of consumers when we factor for attention. I'd even extend the argument to say that this metric is product based in the B2B world, but it's more of a brand measure in the B2C world.

We can uncover some pretty glaring truths about our marketing messaging by clearly understanding who is deep in research mode. For example, if you suddenly have a spike in site visits and awareness based on a successful search engine optimization (SEO) effort, then you'll want to model out a corresponding lift in sales, provided your nurture efforts are up to par.

And the beauty of measuring your consideration level (or activity level, or whatever your business should call it) is that it delivers an objective analysis on how well your nurture strategy is working. Are you effectively—and repeatedly—engaging users to the point of purchase? In a pure B2B setting, is marketing reliably producing sales-qualified leads (SQLs) that close within 60 days or are leads being lost in the process?

(*Note:* For a significantly deeper dive on the B2B sales process [and terms like SQL], I'd suggest consuming the thinking of SiriusDecisions.)

Raving Fans

Although once limited to cult topics like Star Wars or comic books, the idea of identifying and quantifying your best customers truly gained traction with the rise of brand-based loyalty programs. By creating somewhat arbitrary levels of importance (think Silver, Gold, Platinum, Diamond in the Delta Air Lines SkyMiles world), we as marketers have done a decent job at stack-ranking our audiences and understanding how to better meet the wants and desires of each customer type.

The two insights most great loyalty marketers understand is that they should address each of their segments differently—and that most often, the top tier is the most profitable customer for any given business. So by laying out a customer-tiering model, the brightest marketers are, in essence, selecting for the most profitable audiences, which we'll call raving fans.

The beauty of marketing to this elite group is that you can set aside all the simple messaging and introductory content; there's absolutely zero lowest-common-denominator messaging required here. This is the moment to go massively personalized and hyperfocused. If you're an airline, look at routes frequented by business travelers and deliver insider-like destination experience details. If you're a software company, dedicate time and effort to build a private community in which your most prolific users can share tips and tricks.

This group makes a perfect starting place for wading into behavioral marketing—especially if you're trying to prove an immediate business case. For example, I know an email marketing director who was under serious pressure to increase her sends from a less-than-enlightened VP. She warned that increasing sends to her audience could have a negative effect on the overall health of her program. Although she was exactly correct from a best-practices standpoint, that did not assuage her management.

So when forced to send more email, she came up with a solution only a great data-driven marketer would conceive. She tripled the monthly volume to her most active and best customers—with the hopes that their brand advocacy would blunt any negative effects on deliverability. But a funny thing happened when the volume went up—so did her opens, clicks, and CLV. She inadvertently discovered even more latent desire to hear from her ecommerce brand, and was rewarded with a nice lift in sales.

The moral of the story is that we should all segment for and test aggressively with our best customers. If you're winning with a specific set of recipients, then clearly explore the limits of that fandom. Consider how many million people receive Groupon or other deal site emails at least once a day, yet only redeem a tiny percentage of them. That deal-seeking persona is more than willing to sort through the volume to find the golden nugget. Most marketers aren't Groupon, but thinking about increasing communications to your best customers might be the smartest short-term test going.

Disinterested Recipients

At the complete opposite end of the spectrum from raving fans are those who are utterly disinterested in your marketing messaging. This can take many forms, ranging from not interacting with mail communications for months, to not purchasing anything for years.

Although email as a channel doesn't carry an expensive cost-per-piece price tag the way direct or call centers do, it most certainly is not free—especially if your list is in the hundreds of thousands. The price for not doing email well is, in fact, much more expensive than just cutting a check to a vendor. The penalty comes in the form of ISP blacklists, SPAM traps, and general deliverability problems. If you just keep blasting away in batch send mode to a disinterested list of recipients, you will absolutely find yourself in some hot water—both internally from poor marketing performance, and externally with deliverability entities like Spamhaus.

The simplest way to avoid this pain is to define your inactive users upfront and lay out an automated way to deal with disinterested recipients across the board. From a best-practices perspective, most great brands set the specific behaviors and time constraints—for example, no email opens for eight months plus no purchases for 12 months. Or if you want a slightly higher bar that requires actions beyond email opens, you might set the rule to no email clicks within six months plus no buy-page site views for 12 months.

Once a user reaches this combination of objective rules, they should be suppressed from all existing bulk campaigns and dropped into a reactivation nurture program. Although I'd recommend taking these users out of all queries for large mailings, I normally leave them eligible for my most behavior-driven campaigns. If they suddenly show up on my site, put three high-value items in their cart but don't checkout, I certainly wouldn't want a rule to suppress them out of receiving the cart abandon email.

Once they're segmented away from the larger population, now is the time to outline the best possible rescue strategy. This can manifest very differently with offers and discounts depending on your business; but in general, the program should be at least three touches across 75 to 90 days. If you're an aggressive ecommerce retailer, your first message might be a 10 percent off coupon, the second might be a 25 percent off coupon, and the third should almost always be the same: a singular-focused ask for a click to remain in the program. For a longer-lead, single-purchase scenario, you might have longer inactive windows—and the messages might be more focused on interacting with other channels such as taking a car into a service department or upgrading to the latest version of a software package.

The best performing rescue campaigns reactivate somewhere around 10 percent of recipients, so make sure to set your expectations correctly going in. One great nurture program will not make up for a series of less-than-stellar marketing touches over time. Ideally, you should be measuring how many people enter this rescue nurture program as a top-line measure of the overall health of your email program. I know some very successful email marketers who check the counts on those campaigns weekly as part of their expanded KPI reporting dashboard.

Although the expense of other channels like direct mail and call centers reduce our desire to take a big cost hit to reactive disinterested customers, there's one very important exception. For the highest-value customers who fall off the radar—either by a lack of qualifying behavior or via an email opt-out—these other channels can be a great kick-save opportunity. Maybe some process glitch created their opt-out (Dad forwards email to Mom, who clicks the opt-out which was specific to Dad) or they've just moved beyond that stage in their life (a previous diaper purchaser who now has a 4-year-old no longer wearing them). But once you've created raving fans, fight hard to retain them. Dropping a postcard or an outbound telesales call with a clear call to action (including filling out a survey as a last result) can be an effective way to demonstrate your dedication to that specific customer relationship, which can be all it takes to reactivate a recipient.

Percentage of Completed Records

Finally, I'll include a more CRM-like measurement into the mix because it's equally important for marketers of any product or service. Quantifying the depth of your data at the record level can be an incredibly effective way of measuring your success. For example, if you have a traditional database keyed on an email address, you can easily quantify how many records have one more field (first name, for example), two more fields (first name + last name), three more fields (first name + last name + postal code), and so on.

Not only does this give you a depth analysis of your data; it also helps guide any data append efforts you might undertake either via offline partnerships and service providers—or directly with your recipients via forms wrapped around content or with event registrations. You should truly be thinking about how each customer interaction adds to the quality of your data, and making sure you get your half of the value exchange powered by great content strategy.

We discussed anonymous users in Chapter 9, which is an equally good measure to track. How many anonymous users does your marketing automation system track weekly? How many convert into named prospects in your database? And, maybe, most anecdotally interesting, which content pieces are most likely to drive this registration?

I like to add seemingly random KPIs like this to an overall view of a program, because they provide an important second-order window into your effort. There's no absolute right or wrong answer for how deep your data should be, but having a metric begins the process of improvement. You might have a stated goal to have an average of 4.5 fields of data per customer record by the end of the fiscal year, and, therefore, you'd be willing to think about data append efforts as a mainstream program as opposed to some organic event that just happens.

With almost all these emerging measurements, there's one objective technology piece underlying all this goodness: scoring. The chapter will end with a deep dive on this topic, but it's important to understand that almost every measure we discussed earlier requires us to break behaviors and actions down into their smallest component pieces, and then score each one individually.

When we combine each score (both positive and negative) with the concept of time, we get to a quantified view of an element like raving fans. We might say they represent anyone with an activity score above 500 and at least one purchase in the last six months and a CLV above $200.

The only way to measure these elements over time is to make them the base of a beautifully orchestrated scoring model. More on that in a minute.

Being Your Own Harshest Critic

Before we dive into the mother of all measurement and optimization techniques, let's spend a moment celebrating one of my favorite human traits: constructive dissatisfaction. Some of the most successful marketers I know are in relentless pursuit of the "next big thing." They design their campaigns to be measurable from the beginning. They also have ultrafocused testing parameters, which means they wring the strongest results out of a manageable set of tests. They internalize the company's marketing and sales goals, and help their internal customers hit those numbers.

There's also a corresponding set of things they *don't* do. They don't ask permission to improve their programs. They don't overtest and underdeliver. They don't wait for the business to tell them what to do. They don't let perfect be the enemy of good.

In this way, the strongest marketers are their own harshest critics. They understand it's almost always better to present solutions and marketing opportunities to their business partners as opposed to standard reports on requested activities. They reframe the success criteria around more meaningful elements, and they relentlessly explore new tactics.

I see this approach work at almost every level. In fact, I remember a director-level friend who ran a huge ecommerce business in the early 2000s telling me he proactively held back 10 percent of his budget to support pure innovation experiments. He was thinking deeply about driving repeat purchase and other key ecommerce goals 12 to 14 years ago, and was willing to test and explore with many on- and off-line strategies—even working with very early stage startups who were equally as early in thinking about data-driven marketing.

Unsurprisingly, he steadily rose through the ranks over the last decade to VP, and has now parlayed that into another senior executive position externally. The lesson is simple: be bold, dedicate real dollars, and advocate for innovation as aggressively as possible.

When it comes to optimization and high-level performance, almost all the best marketers relentlessly move their own goalposts. No one from sales comes over and asks for a new funnel report on marketing qualified leads to sales qualified leads ratios; it's something a lead-gen driven marketer is already tracking, measuring, and sharing outside their group.

It also comes into clear play during the annual budgeting process. When truly great marketers bring forward next year's budget, they're focused on executing more of what was successful last year, and less of what was mediocre. And although it sounds straightforward, it's almost never that easy. Great marketers are always in search of flexible budget allocations and external programs that drive exponential revenue for incrementally more investment. We're moving toward a world in which preprogramming marketing campaigns or events 6 to 12 months in advance just won't be the most effective way to market.

Let's say you run a successful ecommerce business selling crafting supplies to 25- to 40-year-old women, and Pinterest launches a brand new sponsored content advertising product in the second quarter next year. Do you want your marketing dollars already committed to print advertising or do you want to double-down on Pinterest because it's already driving a ton of sales conversions—and it's directly measureable?

By being as constructively dissatisfied as humanly possible in your role, you'll set the tone for both measurement and optimization of all your programs. You'll be the one starting the conversation on alternate KPIs—not the MBA that just got hired into a product analyst role.

Scoring: The Holy Grail of Objective Measurement

If all this micro measurement and ranking sounds like pure gibberish, and you have no idea where to start or how to proceed, hang on. The great news is that you can bring all your measurement and optimization strategies to life using one simple concept: scoring.

Broken down to its simplest concept, scoring allows us to assign (and subtract) points to a deep series of small events, and then sum them in real-time to add an entirely new layer of information to a record in our database. Although scoring was traditionally a preferred tactic of B2B marketers trying to quantify the likelihood of a prospect closing during a months- or years-long sales process, it's now absolutely commonplace across B2C as well as a measure of activity level and CLV. Almost every element or behavior associated with our prospect or customer can have points assigned—and can contribute to a scoring model.

It's also important to recognize that we might have two or three or four concurrent scoring models running at any given time. Although they may trend in similar directions (imagine that more active users will likely translate into more repeat customers provided your marketing is effective), each scoring model may be radically different and unassociated with all other scores.

For example, I know software companies who sell traditional package software with a customer-satisfaction score that is maintained across channels and over time. The most recognizable of these might be the Net Promoter Score concept that came out of *Harvard Business Review* in 2003. Satmetrix, one of the innovators of the method, describes it this way:

> The Net Promoter Score, or NPS®, is based on the fundamental perspective that every company's customers can be divided into three categories: Promoters, Passives, and Detractors.
>
> By asking one simple question—How likely is it that you would recommend [your company] to a friend or colleague?—you can track these groups and get a clear measure of your company's performance through your customers' eyes. Customers respond on a 0- to 10-point rating scale and are categorized as follows:
>
> - Promoters (score 9–10) are loyal enthusiasts who will keep buying and refer others, fueling growth.
>
> - Passives (score 7–8) are satisfied but unenthusiastic customers who are vulnerable to competitive offerings.
>
> - Detractors (score 0–6) are unhappy customers who can damage your brand and impede growth through negative word-of-mouth.
>
> To calculate your company's NPS, take the percentage of customers who are Promoters and subtract the percentage who are Detractors.

Companies most often pose these NPS questions via Interactive Voice Reponses (IVR) systems in a post-call session or via email. Although measuring both the score and the subjective input associated with the score (the latter turns out to be the really hard part of making the data meaningful and actionable), this exercise often becomes so high level that it's rendered ineffective. Marketing can blame product for not including all the required features for strong NPS scores, and sales can blame support just as easily for not effectively dealing with customer concerns that lead to fewer repeat buyers. Although it's a solid framework to think about across your entire organization, be prepared for the process itself to create some great internal drama in the first year of rollout.

Conversely, we can think about scoring at a much more marketing-specific level. The concept of behavioral marketing really catches fire when we begin to consider how to score an active customer. For example, we might lay out an ecommerce model like this:

Email open: 5 points.

Email click: 10 points.

No Email opens for a month: –10 points.

Browse shopping-oriented site page: 10 points.

Unsolicited site visit: 20 points.

Click buy now in an Email: 25 points.

Cart an item: 40 points.

Abandon a cart: –40 points.

Generate a transaction (below $50): 100 points.

Generate a transaction (above $50): 150 points.

CLV above $500: 250 points

Once you run the models for a few weeks, it'll become very clear how each individual ranks among the masses. You'll now have a unique activity score on every record in your database, and can begin to individually market to bands of these customers.

Thinking back to our earlier discussion on raving fans and disinterested recipients, your baseline scores might be above 300 and below 50, respectively. Once you've got individual users rolled into bands, you can begin hyperfocused marketing based on where they lie in the spectrum. You can try to effectively market items related to a recent purchase for the most active users or get them to visit a retail store if they've only ever purchased online. Your goal might be to engage the least active in one of your two to three content streams and begin to earn back some credibility by becoming a trusted source of information. Either way, you can see that quantifying the effort via a scoring model is the great differentiator.

And speaking of multiple scoring models, I know many groups outside marketing who look to quantify their users. Most commonly, call centers will maintain customer satisfaction indices based on how often someone calls, whether the company resolves their issues quickly and what their NPS score is. Understanding how marketing's efforts fit into these other scoring models is just as critical as deriving your own. By providing more data points to enrich other groups' views will earn you the good will needed to round out your own scoring models.

Although I could literally write another 5,000 words on scoring models, it boils down to this: get yourself a world-class SaaS tool that manages a solid level of scoring events and just get started. You don't even have to act on them for four to six months if you don't have the bandwidth, but the longer they're running—and you're tuning them— the more effectively they will support your data-driven decisions in the future. You can push, pull, and experiment with scoring models in the background of your marketing effort until you're supremely com-fortable with your approach, and then simply factor them into your segmentation criteria, build dynamic content for specific segments, and you're off and running.

Conclusion

Although measurement and optimization can mean different things to every marketer, the goal here is to expand your thinking and introduce some deeper criteria to consider beyond simple channel-specific methods like open rate or click-through rate. More often than not, those who think most critically about measurement end up with the best performing programs. I believe this is a combination of old-fashioned critical thinking powered by deeper data and a marketer's natural sense of restlessness.

It should go without saying that each of your specific channels should be operating at near-peak performance—especially those that are very expensive or occur at large scale. The old adage about things worth doing are worth doing right should be your mantra here. Nail the basics of your channel-level performance, ensure you're aggressively maintaining the high quality of work via optimization, and then apply the five emerging views we discussed above—or define your own that fit perfectly into your business. Your marketing game will rise quickly, and in almost every customer case I see, your revenue contribution will rise as well.

Part Three
Success Beyond the Behavioral Marketing Basics

13 It's All About the Team

Staffing the Right Players to Succeed

In Part One of the book (Chapters 1–4), we covered topics like roles, people, and technology related to embracing behavioral marketing as a discipline. And in Part Two (Chapters 5–12), we focused on putting behavioral marketing into action across all your channels. Now, let's dive a couple of levels deeper as we move beyond the basics and get to driving real change within your marketing organization in the final five chapters.

The Marketer Persona

First, let's focus on some key attributes we as marketers tend to have. Although it may not apply to every marketer you've ever met, we are largely an aspirational, driven and hard-working group—typically not very good at saying no. We skew younger in age because the pace early in our career is typically insane and full of 80-hour weeks and responsibility that exceeds the number of years we've been on the planet. (For example—I was 25 with 10 people reporting to me, and had about $2M of annual P&L on my head.)

Those early years are critically foundational for a marketer. You choose your area of specialty—ad agency or digital, when I was coming up—and hopefully build your early experience working with some of the best minds in your executive structure. You learn quickly whether you're more comfortable in the multiclient chaos of the agency world, or if you perform best when deeply immersed into a single brand and working in corporate. You also normally delineate between being a marketing practitioner or a people manager. Some people just love marketing execution in their soul, but others are focused on getting promoted and managing people. Neither is right or wrong; you just have to figure out where you feel more comfortable. Finding a candidate who has an equal passion for both is like running across a rainbow unicorn—grab it quickly, and be prepared to nurture and protect it for years!

Another powerful trait among marketers is that we're pretty good estimators of all sorts of things—response rates, people's intentions, salespeople's BS quotient, campaign success, and so forth. This certainly is a skill we build over time, but I find even the youngest marketers among us have the passion to pay close attention to how *they're* marketed to, and be able to take cues and data from that experience. They may not be able to logically defend their choices, but gut instinct is doubtlessly part of being a great marketer. I often tell mid-level marketers that they're probably way better predictors than they think they are, and when concocting A/B tests to make sure the two choices are almost diametrically opposed.

Interestingly enough, marketers also tend to take a bit of dramatic license—especially when describing how busy they are. This doesn't mean that every marketing department has all the staff it needs; but almost every marketer I talk to has no idea how they'll make time to do anything differently. I'm going to peg that quotient at 70 percent true, and 30 percent of it is the result of us being creative people with a slightly elevated self-worth.

And finally, we're almost all relatively social beings. No group inside a company throws a Halloween party like marketing, right? (Except maybe sales.) Everyone dresses up. People sneak alcohol in. There's a predefined after-party spot already picked out. We love to have fun—both at work and at play—and we're pretty good at blurring the lines between the two.

I offer this in-depth persona for two specific reasons: (1) self-awareness is an amazing trait, and knowing how others perceive us can be worth its weight in gold; and (2) these attributes are exactly the motivational factors that marketing leadership needs to understand and index toward. After all, knowing is half the battle, right?

Two Key Traits: Potential and Grit

So how do we use this information about how we work to more effectively build out marketing teams? Firstly, as I emphasized in Chapter 3—focus on potential. Hiring director-level talent is about pure performance and people-management skills, but you should view everyone below that level through the lens of a single question: "How great could they be with the right guidance?"

That assumes two important facts: (1) you have the right managers to deliver the best guidance; and (2) the individual can capably manage the basic responsibilities of the role. This doesn't mean you should hire the smartest aeronautical engineer to run your database marketing team because both roles thrive on great math skills, but it's essential to be flexible in a great candidate's direct work experience and your job requirements. Maybe that overly extroverted database manager you just interviewed would be a great numbers- and process-driven social media manager. Or maybe that amazing email marketing manager you just interviewed is really the person to take you into the future of behavioral marketing at the director level, and you're about to have to make a tough decision about who leads that function in your group.

The other reason to hire on potential is the best way to build an epic top-to-bottom team is to "raise 'em like you want 'em." You're always going to face the cost pressures of retaining great talent at the director level, so why not build out a corporate version of a baseball farm team? Make training and mentorship a key role of your managers, and build an environment that generates brilliance by design. You'll gain a reputation as a great place to work (and, yes, all those socially active marketers talk all the time about new places to work), and you'll maximize the time you have with the brightest candidates you can find and develop.

The other attribute I sought out was an intangible I didn't quite know how to articulate before I attended a marketing leadership roundtable event put on by the Corporate Executive Board in late 2012. That was where I was introduced to the term *grit*. The CEB summarized the definition like this:

> Focusers win because they have "grit"—the ability to overcome adversity to reach higher-order goals:
>
> - Gritty people (e.g., focusers) are defined by an extraordinary ability to stay focused on higher-order goals and overcome challenges to achieve them.
> - Gritty people are particularly successful in unstructured, ambiguous, and challenging environments.
> - In fact, grit is the strongest predictor of success in many environments—above and beyond the impact of IQ and other positive traits.

I wrote an entire blog post about the topic (http://bit.ly/grittymarketers) soon after returning from that event. It outlines the concept at a much deeper level—and links to the primary research in its entirety. I summarized it like this:

> The most important takeaway for me was you don't need (or want) someone who can give the perception of riding every wave — the most effective players are the ones who can see the longer game, prioritize the solutions and execute to the end.

So go figure out what *grit* means to you and to your hiring and professional development effort.

Making Great Marketing Managers

I'm no HR guru, but I can add a bit more detail on hiring and grooming great managers—primarily because I used to hang a lot of responsibility on them to manage employees with great potential into strong team players.

First of all, if you're executing perfectly, you should be promoting your managers from your internal groups. Everyone should understand the importance of mentoring and training exactly like the mentoring and training they received. Short of that perfection, I'm always looking for someone I believe can excel in the manager role—which is the absolute point of marketing execution.

A director or VP must ensure—even demand—that the manager spends time developing their people; and I don't mean weekly 15-minute standing meetings to talk through program status, I mean at least an hour a week in pure mentoring where manager-level tasks, data points, and thought processes are discussed in a two-way interactive format. Believe me, you want a great manager to create another great manager to ensure continuity over time (and to save you a lot of time wasted during a typical hiring process), and building that into the manager's role is positive for both the manager and direct report.

Marketing is not a game that's won by the brilliant loner in the corner who uncovers some ancient secret to more effective response rates. It's most successful when it's out in the glorious sunlight—when you communicate strategy, empower and expect people to contribute, and the team shares the wins.

If that sounds kind of too idealistic or altruistic, remember you're dealing with a generation that's now much more concerned with being challenged and happy at their job than they are with the hours they work. Harness that power to become an employer of choice for the smartest rising managers and interns coming out of the best universities close to you, and you'll be significantly more successful in your own career.

14 Managing Upwards

Socialize If You Must, Prove Results Every Time

Although the previous chapter focused on how to gear up and nurture the right team in order to bring behavioral marketing to life, this chapter provides a how-to exercise for the single practitioner or tiny team. This thinking is designed for the marketer who has a decent, if old-school, management structure that's not necessarily going to help you much strategically. These marketers certainly want better campaign-level performance and revenue lift, but they aren't going to be much help in getting there. This is a unique scenario that requires both an expert touch and a clear understanding of results-oriented internal positioning.

Two-thirds of the effort is recognizing the challenge ahead, and that recognition should be a major factor in how you move forward. Although other peers are going to have a smoother road forward than you, that doesn't mean you can't also make great progress. I've personally seen more than one marketer who figured out how to bring behavioral marketing to life in an overly hostile environment and then went on to massive success at a different company. It wasn't necessarily a walk in the park, but accomplishing that in a subpar environment simply emboldened them the next time out, when they clearly selected a more supportive environment.

Seeing the Tree among the Forest

So what are the leading indicators that you're going to be swimming upstream against in your effort to bring behavioral marketing into your company? Initially, I'd consider how much your firm invests in marketing headcount. Typically, the fewer people your company has in marketing (commensurate with the size of the business), the harder your road is going to be.

You can look at the simple ratio of sales people to marketing people. Again, it depends a lot on your business model, but generally I see ratios of about five to eight sellers for every marketer for mature sellers that have a blend of marketing-based demand generation and sales-based closing.

It's also a warning sign if you've got one to two marketing people in total, whereas the sales group has continually grown past 10, 20, or 30 in the last year. That should be a clue your management team is very much focused on revenue growth but aren't truly understanding the geometric progression that happens when sales and marketing are working well together.

Finally, you should be able to take quick stock of your executives' skill level and familiarity with the discipline of marketing. If they believe your success hangs on great writing, pretty pictures, and good product-slick design, then know you're going to be pushing a decent-sized rock up a big hill. Be prepared to inform and educate your direct boss—or potentially your entire executive team—based on already-achieved milestones and simplistic business terms. Said crassly, you're going to have to dumb it down pretty significantly.

Where to Begin When You're Alone

If you're stuck in this unfortunate spot, I recommend a couple things right away. First, go find some local peers who are in similar-sized companies or the same industry. You can normally find them hanging out at local chapters of national groups such as the American Marketing Association or the Interactive Marketing Association; you can also look for groups on LinkedIn or work your own network to find similar people in related roles around town.

This step is critical because sometimes you're going to need a sounding board when building tests or defining campaign rules. In fact, I would be seeking to add this kind of knowledge to your own personal network immediately for two critical reasons: (1) support along your current journey, and (2) as a means for finding your next job at a more progressive company.

Second, I'd spend even more time upfront planning your journey, its milestones, and your own personal off ramp. Know that it's going to be difficult, and plan your exit upfront. This might sound harsh, but your optimism and job satisfaction can be ground down pretty quickly, and life's too short to absolutely hate your job. Pledge to yourself that you'll give it a 125 percent effort for a decent amount of time, and evaluate your progress honestly.

You'll remember that I spoke in Chapter 4 about how young marketers are often promoted by changing jobs; now's the time to experiment, learn, and prepare for your next role. What would you want to tell your next employer you achieved while working so hard to increase marketing performance in this insanely hostile environment?

Plan Less, Experiment More, and Document Everything

Now that you've accepted the challenge and set some personal boundaries, it's time to develop your approach. This might sound diametrically opposed to what I just said about taking more time up front, but I would spend less time actually laying out your plan. No one's going to need or want to see the fully blown plan before you begin executing, so why start down the path of analysis paralysis?

Accept that this is one of the few benefits you'll have with a hands-off executive team, but recognize that it also means you're probably working with a fixed budget and all the resources you're going to have. In other words, you must prove the business case later when you want to increase paid media spend or headcount—but at least you don't have to get everything pre-approved.

And on the subject of approvals, don't worry about gaining many up front. Rather, recognize with utter clarity that you need to execute solidly. Even if you figured out the ideal terms to describe your process and thinking, it's still going to fly 20,000 feet over their head. Your job is to maintain your executives' trust and continue to produce great results. The secret is you're working on a way to drive results 10 times the great ones of the past, but don't be foolish enough to try to convince them up front. Walk the walk; forget the talk.

Even though you're going to spend less time concocting ROI models and business cases up front, that doesn't mean you can attack the tasks with any less rigor. In fact, you should clearly recognize you're fighting a pretty big battle all by yourself, which means you'll need maximum creativity and to be testing far and wide across your tactics. Your appetite to experiment should far exceed what a traditional marketing manager who has weekly meetings with their boss would think about.

You must also prepare for all the harrowing moments when top-line performance dips a bit because you're testing that aggressively or when your budget doesn't grow year over year because sales slowed down based on market factors (not because of you cratering the sales function, which you'd better not ever even get close to!).

You must transfer the effort you would have normally spent upfront into an exacting focus on tracking, reporting, and analysis on the back side of your campaigns. There will come a point when you will need to convince an old-school boss that your new-school approach is better, faster, and creates more sales for the same investment, and you need to have the data to back up your assertion.

The problem is that you don't know exactly when that's going to happen. You may never get called out that aggressively or you might have to defend your entire budget, marketing approach, and core existence next Wednesday in the CEO's office. You must always have that business-proof case ready, so start early and keep that supersmart, concise PowerPoint deck constantly refreshed.

Knowing You've Won or Lost

Because this is such a tenuous effort, you've got to set some time- and sanity-based parameters. Otherwise, you're likely to fall into a dysfunctional rhythm with your dysfunctional company and will, therefore, waste very precious time in your career. Oddly enough, I believe this is more important the earlier you are in your career. You'll never get those formative years back, and you've got to hustle very fast early on to find your place in the work world.

If you manage to successfully integrate behavioral marketing thinking in this scenario and you've dragged an old-school group (somewhat quietly) kicking and screaming into the digital age, then *that's* an epic accomplishment. You might have just figured out your calling: driving change management and performance lift into old-school marketing teams. Congratulations! You now have a skill you can build on for the rest of your marketing career.

If, on the other hand, you gave it your best shot for a year or through a couple of product launches and your executives are just as clueless as when you began, it's time to throw in the proverbial towel. But keep in mind that the customer focus and behavioral aspects you were able to execute improved the situation and that things are better now than they would have been without your effort.

Get to work on finding a new gig, and keep in mind when attempting to find a more supportive environment that you want to look for the polar opposite of your current fixer-upper of a marketing department. And congratulations! You worked hard, took on a challenge, and truly tried to make things better. You've just injected yourself with a good dose of the grit I also talk about in Chapter 13, which is always a good thing.

Conclusion

Although this was very much geared to the individual practitioner trying to bring behavioral marketing to an old-school marketing group, it probably equally applies to a small group of less than three or four marketers working for a less-than-great marketing team. Maybe the only difference is who you complain to about how backward your company is; the individual likely bores his or her significant other, and the team probably spends lots of happy hours and lunches disparaging the situation.

Either way, changing the course of a marketing department is a tall order. There are often significant forces at play that keep things operating as they always have. For some, change is scary and create some existential questions like "Can I still be good at my job if it's changed this much?" Understanding the reason behind some of the pushback can be an eye-opening realization, and working around it elegantly can be the difference between failure and success.

So whether you're a single practitioner or a small group, I'd suggest you meet this challenge head on with action. Know that your best chance is to understand the existing expectations, and spend every minute of effort above those expectations on blowing them out of the water. Check the boxes on your everyday job while plotting an undeniable future state of marketing that's built around your customers' needs and is dynamic based on your customers' actions. Even if it doesn't work out at today's gig, it's killer training for the future.

15 Best Friend Brands

Becoming Indispensable to Your Customer

A real-world example of what behavioral marketing success looks like at the campaign and marketer level is Silverpop's sponsored primary research into a concept we call Best Friend Brands. Generally these are a user's most important 5 to 10 brand relationships. We wanted to document how users thought about their top brands and how a brand can truly make their way into their customer's inner circle. We surveyed almost 4,000 people across the United States, the United Kingdom, and Germany to ensure we have a well-represented global view and diverse email interaction types.

One of the core truths in regard to the ability of humans to interact socially is that we are limited by the number of people we can interact with efficiently. British anthropologist and evolutional psychologist Robin Dunbar has theorized that the maximum number is 150. As head of the Social and Evolutionary Neuroscience Research Group in the Department of Experimental Psychology at the University of Oxford, Dunbar has some amazing credibility. He defines his Dunbar's number as:

> A measurement of the cognitive limit to the number of individuals with whom any one person can maintain stable relationships.

That maximum of 150 shows up in all kinds of unique ways. It might be your complete extended-friend group when you were in your mid-twenties and single. Or it might be your friends plus your extended family if you're in your late thirties and married with children. We also see this thinking exhibited in today's social networking applications—specifically the photo sharing application Path, which differentiates from other photo-sharing apps by limiting the size of your sharing audience to 150 for exactly the reason Robin Dunbar outlines.

After discovering that there's a natural limit of 150, think about what it takes to be in the top 5 percent of that realm from a brand perspective. What does it mean to trust a brand so deeply that you interact seamlessly across three or four channels? How strong is the connection with an ecommerce brand if a recipient opens almost every email sent and buys two to three times per quarter? Getting to the attributes behind this type of advocacy is an interesting study in core tenets of behavioral marketing.

This chapter walks you through my personal Top 5 Best Friend Brands along with a detailed look at why I find them so compelling. At times, it's the channel-level excellence such as a perfect song recommendation from Spotify via email, but other days it's a cross-channel highly personalized experience that wins thousands of dollars in revenue from me annually.

Before we plunge into the brands themselves, let me provide a quick overview of the research's high points. You can read the entire study here at http://bit.ly/BFBWhitePaper—which, incidentally, I've provided as a direct link without the need for you to opt in to our nurture marketing to get. That's a textbook example of a content strategy perfectly in play—an interested audience member consumes top-level information that includes a link to a deeper content piece. However, accessing that deeper piece would typically require the user to be opted in to nurture marketing communication. So the user receives the value of expert thinking on a topic, and the marketer earns the right to continue the conversation and potentially end up making a sale. But no opt in is required here to read and share away—you gloriously anonymous user!

From a numbers perspective, the Best Friend Brands research outlined the following realities:

- The average number of Best Friend Brands is 4.5.

- The average pace of online purchases is one per month, so it's critical to be timely in your marketing messaging.

- 71 percent of consumers would be more likely to make a purchase if the initial email outreach from a retailer or brand had been tailored especially to them (and was a full 10 points higher in Germany).

- 58 percent of consumers said they wouldn't even open an email if they thought it irrelevant to them or their needs.

- 40 percent of consumers wouldn't open an email if the subject line wasn't relevant to them.

- 64 percent of people would open an email simply because they trusted the brand.

- More than 25 percent of respondents said that a brand's email approach had stopped them from buying.

- 34 percent of respondents said they would leave emails unopened if they receive too much correspondence from the brand.

- 17 percent of the people surveyed said they tend to purchase directly from a brand email once a month (which rose to 21 percent in the United States).

- 67 percent of consumers want to receive information, such as new products, special offers, transactional information and newsletter via email.

The takeaway for all these numbers comes back to one of the core tenets of behavioral marketing: relevance and trust are absolute keys to a great marketing effort. This study looked mostly at the email channel, but you'll see when I share my own Top 5 Best Friend Brands that it's a much more holistic, cross-channel experience that drives massive advocacy.

My Best Friend Brands

I normally don't use myself (or my inbox) as an example because sometimes my job makes me overly critical or interested in tiny aspects of email campaigns that few others would ever care about. So I was really surprised when a few talks I gave on Best Friend Brands became highly interactive after taking a deep dive into my own relationship with these brands. I think it's because so often we talk about marketing—and specifically behavioral marketing—in such general terms that it can seem overly theoretical or not directly applicable to what happens in your inbox every day. So let's jump right in.

Number Five: Spotify

The music streaming company Spotify is brilliant because they understand the role that online music plays in my world: pure new artist discovery. Music is a central part of both my work and home life. As I write this section, I'm listening to Mirella Freni and Luciano Pavarotti's 1987 Decca recording of Puccini's La Boheme on 11. I've explored many more Puccini and Donizetti operas to hone my ear for both tenors and sopranos. I've also rediscovered some old musical friends like Mogwai and Daft Punk while writing this book, as well as unearthing some new up-and-coming talent like UK singer/songwriter James Bay.

The beauty is that Spotify both allows and suggests that I listen to multiple versions of the same opera but also understands the recommendation engine should behave differently when it's pop music. In these instances, it sees me listening to new music (Chvrches, for example, as shown in Figure 15.1) and recommends other new music that's similar.

One of the benefits of being so personalized all the time is that Spotify has earned the right to send me suggestions that might be driven by attributes beyond my musical taste. For example, I got the email

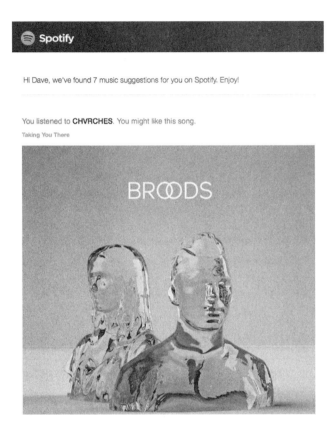

Figure 15.1 Spotify's Recommendation Engine Is Based on Listener Behaviors

shown in Figure 15.2 for an artist I'd never heard of named Yuna. It's not explicitly stated that it's recommended based on my listening habits, so I assume it could very well have been paid marketing done by her record company or even an Editor's Pick from the staff at Spotify. Either way, I still go listen.

For this amazing depth of personalized recommendations—and even deeper brilliance like my very own "Year in Music" campaign (see Figure 15.3), Spotify drives content relevance like few other brands in my inbox. (And yes, go listen to Eli "Paperboy" Reed if you love Philly-style pop soul.)

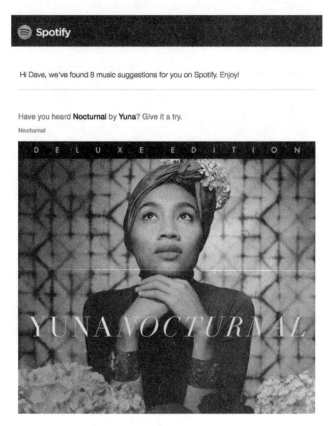

Figure 15.2 Even Without Specific Listening Behaviors, Spotify Recommends Featured Artists

Number Four: GILT Group

Although those who know me wouldn't really use the phrase "fashion forward," I do actually pay attention to clothing and accessories and even dress myself without much help from my wife. My blue Steve Madden wingtips tend to get a few fun comments every time I step on stage. When it comes to shopping for these items, my favorite email relationship by far is with GILT.

Although I only buy two or three times a year, I really enjoy consuming GILT's email content for one very specific reason: all the key brands are smartly placed in the subject line. Does this virtually destroy

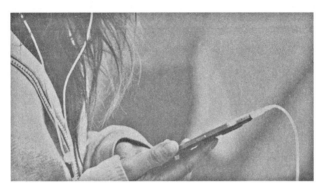

Hi

Your top song of 2014 was Just Like Me
by Eli Paperboy Reed.

Want to know more? Check out the rest of your Year in Music now.

Figure 15.3 The Top Song in My "Year in Music"

the old rules around 40-character subject lines? Absolutely. Do I look at every single one that lands in my inbox? Again—absolutely.

When I receive content like the message shown in Figure 15.4 that contains brands I love (Tumi Luggage is visible, and John Varvatos and Hickey Freeman are below the fold), I often average 8 to 10 opens and clicks per message as I look at items and availability more than once. And when I buy, it's typically not a $15 pair of socks. Suffice it to say I'm a good value proposition for GILT.

From a user experience perspective, I love how this class of ecommerce sellers has pioneered an elegant way for me to skip campaigns that contain brands I don't care about. They were the first brands to completely jettison the old 40-character subject line best-practices

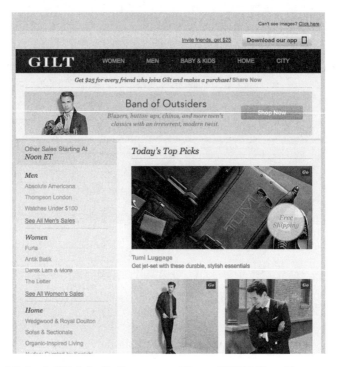

Figure 15.4 A Highly-Relevant-to-Dave GILT Email

rule, and began jamming every featured brand into the subject line. For example, I received this subject line just today:

> Vintage Finds Feat. What Goes Around Comes Around, Costume National: Up to 70% Off, Porsamo Bleu Watches and More Start Today at 9pm ET

That's amazingly specific, and it'd just barely fit in a Tweet or an SMS message at 137 characters. So when I receive a campaign like the one shown in Figure 15.5 featuring brands or products I'm not interested in (Eastland Shoes and Versace watches), I can delete it from my inbox quickly and efficiently.

I may not be GILT Group's most frequent customer, but I'm an incredibly active email user. Often, that exact activity is a great indicator for transaction-level behavior. So for their understanding of making

Figure 15.5 A Considerably Less-Relevant-to-Dave GILT Email

content scannable and shopping simple—and also being very good at brand and SKU selection—GILT is a fixture in my Top 5 brands.

Number Three: eBags

When you travel as much as I do, a go-to retailer for luggage and travel accessories is a must-have, and eBags is my personal favorite. Beyond specializing in items my wife swears I buy like Carrie Bradshaw buys shoes, eBags has honed an incredibly personal stream of content for me. And it absolutely proves the fact that a Best Friend Brand can send five to seven campaigns a week and retain strong engagement.

As you'd expect, eBags is good at cart abandonment emails and even sends me an extra message if the price of an item I've carted drops. Beyond that, it also has browse abandon campaigns set up on a brand-

Figure 15.6 A Browse Abandon Email from eBags Featuring Samsonite Products

by-brand basis, as you can see from the Samsonite message in Figure 15.6 that followed my web-based session by about two hours. Pretty brilliant stuff, huh?

While we're talking about great behavioral marketing campaigns, let's look at eBags' cart abandon program (Figure 15.7). The creative itself isn't mind-blowing, but it clearly conveys some very important buying signals: (1) the design mirrors the cart page, so it's clear I can buy quickly without having to relocate the SKU; (2) they're telling me how much branded reward currency I'll earn for this purchase, which is important for multiple purchasers like me; and (3) they're recommending alternatives in case that item was not exactly what I want.

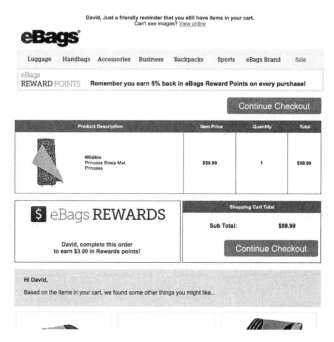

Figure 15.7 EBags Cart Abandon Message

From a cadence perspective, this began within a few hours and continued to run for almost two weeks. It went a bit longer than a normal three-touches-over-two-weeks campaign might run, but eBags gets lots of inbox latitude with me. However, I could see this four-to-five-touch program logic becoming a bit much for other customers who aren't as much as an advocate.

Finally, eBags clearly understands the affinity that's a major behavior driver in the travel industry. Not only does it deliver timely offers and have its own reward currency (which has directly driven a conversion from me in the past); it's affiliated with Delta's SkyMiles Shopping, which gets me even more miles per dollar spent, as shown in Figure 15.8. More on SkyMiles in a minute but suffice to say this is a perfect buying moment for me.

For its aggressive frequency, strong availability of almost any travel-related item, and a clear understanding of my buying drivers, eBags is

Figure 15.8 Delta's SkyMiles Shopping Offer for 10 Miles per Dollar Spent at eBags

my number one pure-play ecommerce brand. And that's saying a lot when you consider what an incredibly crowded segment luggage is from an ecommerce perspective. I could buy from eBags, Amazon, a local department store like Macy's, or direct from the manufacturer. Creating retailer-level buying preference in this scenario by leveraging great behavioral marketing techniques is earning eBags literally millions of dollars annually.

Number Two: Creative Market

Many of my more technical customers are aware that I've been known to hack up an optimized landing page or end up deep in conversation about how best to tackle the age-old question of responsive design for email templates. Although I don't necessarily create assets in Photoshop, I'm a great collector of content from Creative Market—a designer-driven marketplace of fonts, templates, icons, and almost every other asset a designer or developer might need to build beautiful campaigns.

Creative Market absolutely nails the value proposition of our email relationship by delivering a weekly email containing six free asset packs—three on its site, and three on its Facebook page (see Figure 15.9). There are three to four other campaigns every week that educate me on the latest trends and deliver great offers, but the free asset email gets me every time.

In fact, I keep a subdirectory with just those zip files for a rainy day of hacking. So where do you think I go every time I need something beyond the freebies? Yep! I've become a 10- to 15-purchase customer

Figure 15.9 Creative Market's Weekly Free Goods Email

during the last couple of years just by Creative Market engaging me via email.

In addition to powering my infrequent building tasks, Creative Market does an amazing job at updating me on recent design trends. Again, because it's more of a hobby for me, I don't track the latest in logo design or great website templates, but I can follow along with their content, remain up to date, and receive great offers like the one in Figure 15.10.

So for its understanding that trial leads beautifully to purchase, and for keeping me up to date on the latest trends in design, Creative Market is second to only one brand in my inbox. They've crafted an epic value proposition via email that benefits not only their business but also all the artists and designers who sell their products on the site. It's a win–win for both the audience and the marketer, and demonstrates a brand that gets it right on many levels.

Figure 15.10 Creative Market's "What's Hot This Week" Email

Number One: Delta Air Lines

If there's one brand to which I am fanatically loyal, it's Delta Airlines. Given I average somewhere around 175,000 miles annually, I spend an inordinate amount of time planning, booking, and flying—often across multiple channels for every trip. I'm likely to research seat-level availability with a Diamond Medallion desk call center rep, purchase the ticket in my corporate travel portal, modify some aspects of the trip in the mobile app, and then maybe even circle back to the call center preflight. To call me channel agnostic would be a stunning understatement.

Delta understands me at a level most brands couldn't achieve. It knows my notification preferences, and its interactive voice response (IVR) system in the call center recognizes my phone number and routes me to a rep who has my upcoming itineraries on screen before even greeting me (which he or she does by name).

Beyond just the flight experience, Delta builds partnerships with other travel brands like Starwood and Hertz that leverage my Delta status to receive preferred benefits at those other companies. Figure 15.11 shows an example of the Starwood Crossover Reward program that gives me serious hotel-side benefits based on my Diamond Status with Delta. You can imagine how quickly that creates brand preference with my hotels.

Notice how clearly the value proposition is articulated and lays out the benefits. And since this is only available to me because of the segment I'm in within Delta's structure, it is a masterstroke of behavioral marketing by both companies. Delta adds another benefit to its already-strong value proposition, and SPG gets business directly from Delta's most frequent flyers. Very smart co-marketing.

Of course, even your Best Friend Brands can have suboptimal programs. For me, that's Delta's SkyDining program, which earns me a few miles every couple of months but does nothing to affect my choice

Figure 15.11 Starwood Crossover Reward Program

of restaurants (which is what they really are trying to do with the program). The quality and relevance of the locations just isn't up to the standards I consistently receive from Foursquare in terms of reviews and other forms of social proof.

See Figure 15.12 for an example of an email that just misses on the behavioral promise. I don't know these restaurants and they're a fair distance away from my home. This is a case in which building a great behavioral marketing program around a valuable audience has to truly hit on all cylinders. Missing one aspect of it (location selection, in this case) makes the whole program suffer in end-user usefulness.

Figure 15.12 Delta's Less-than-Impressive SkyDining Program

I remain enrolled in SkyDining, however, because they reward you two points for every dollar spent if you're opted in for email versus one point per dollar if you're not. I'm willing to put up with a subpar stream of content in my inbox for the simple 100 percent more earning factor. There's probably a really interesting how-far-can-a-brand-go-to-alien-ate-an-advocate question in this program, but we'll save that one for another day.

The sheer amount of time, money, and effort I spend with Delta Air Lines makes them my clear Number One Best Friend Brand. Delta's service, support, and marketing are strong across virtually all channels, and it makes for an excellent customer experience. Could they do even more things right? Sure, but their game is strong, and if you live in Atlanta and travel, Delta is your choice for many reasons.

Conclusion

In trying to paint a full picture of the benefits of behavioral marketing, I've given you a look deep inside my inbox and my most important brands. Do the same for yourself, and then begin the process of putting your customers in segments as well. You should always have a goal to be among your best customers' Best Friend Brands. That starts with understanding who they are, and continues with building programs, communications, and offers that exceed their expectations.

Some days, these winning programs will mean building great email content and offers, but it might just as easily be something as nondigital as enhancing your call center software to recognize customers by name based on their Caller ID. Start with the simple elements you have complete control over (if someone's shopping beach vacations, *do not* show pictures of Paris in your emails), but chart an aggressive course to make more meaningful change. You're going to need help for lots of other people in your company, but marketing should always be pushing a customer advocacy agenda.

16 Riding the Wave

Career Success Powered by Behavioral Marketing

By now, we've covered the ins and outs of preparing to tackle behavioral marketing, looked at its impact across marketing organizations of all sizes, and have even drilled deeply into how to staff it. We're going to finish with potentially the most individual reason to reorient your marketing effort around behavioral marketing: it'll get you *paid*.

In a world in which entry-level marketing jobs are not easy to land—and finding the right director-level gig is even harder—the best practitioners out there are constantly seeking ways to get the smallest edge. Some are fanatical about professional training, some get an advanced degree or certificate, and some simply define a specialty and seek to be the best in that area.

A Dude Named Rand

To me, this calls to mind the story of Rand Fishkin from Seattle-based search marketing company Moz. Rand began as a 20-something CEO in the search space and has become one of the leading experts in that area even though he turned over day-to-day leadership of the company to a colleague in 2014. His Whiteboard Friday series is the type of educational, value-added brilliant self-promotion that keeps his personal brand top-of-mind and moving forward.

What makes Rand different from any other entry-level marketer, and how did he manage his rise to prominence? Although I don't know him personally, I've been a professional fan of his for years, so I'll give you the abridged "from the outside" version.

Rand originally began working for a digital-marketing-services business his mother owned. They worked together as peers for years, and then Rand stepped in as CEO. From the outside, this move seemed to generally correlate with Moz's efforts to double down on building a scalable product as opposed to running a consulting firm. From there, he created a product that automated the mystical-for-most-people process of great search marketing and built an incredibly strong bootstrap-funded SaaS business. He raised millions of dollars from one of the smartest VCs on the block (Brad Feld of the Foundry Group) and continued to build the business.

Things started to get hairy at that point, and Rand has been amazingly transparent about the challenges he faced. As an entrepreneur by DNA, his posts were incredibly helpful and inspiring as I was going through my own start-up craziness. If you want the full picture, you can read his blog at http://moz.com/rand; but suffice to say they hit a product bump, and delaying new versions was having a rough effect on revenue and morale.

The most interesting aspect of Rand's story is how he came to be such a recognized expert so early, how he brilliantly managed the transition both into and out of the CEO role, and how he's maintained his brand and teachings since then. His story can serve as a blueprint for any marketer.

So if it's hard to get into a great marketing gig, even tougher to keep one, and you normally have to change companies to get promoted, then how do we mitigate all this mess? One of the easiest ways is to dedicate yourself equally to both the art and the science of marketing. If you can predictably drive revenue and your track record for the last two to three years is rock solid, then you're going to get that next great job. It doesn't matter how many people show up with slick presentations and highly designed resumes. Hang your hat on data-driven marketing, and understand the critical role that behaviors play in accurately predicting your customers' purchase behaviors.

Your job is to separate your skills and business results from your peers, and that's true whether you're the specialist or the CMO. The interview committee just looks different. I've seen plenty of incredibly forward-looking VPs become CMOs, and too often they have to go hire an external agency to execute on their amazing vision because the internal staff is two years behind in execution skills. At the same time, I've seen specialists hired straight out of college who are the managers 10 months later and starting to build their personal brand at industry meetings and speaking events.

So what makes behavioral marketing such an effective strategy for propelling this kind of differentiation? The easiest answer is virtually any level of marketing professional can implement some flavor of behavioral marketing—from small campaign improvements done by a manager to a CMO who changes the staffing mix in the group to add data analysis capabilities. The minute you're adding value that drives more revenue, you're on the ideal path.

Your Personal Brand

Although I used this phrase when telling Rand's story, "your personal brand" is something most marketers don't think enough about. So many marketers think they're beyond slammed, and couldn't possibly focus on something as silly as their brand when there's so much other work to do. I often hear the same thing about training and development, which is equally ludicrous. If you don't work hard to level-up your skills and your prominence within your professional community, who's going to do it?

There are literally thousands of ways to get involved with your professional community in this day and age, and that's where your brand building should start. Attend professional meetings, find peers on LinkedIn, and meet your friend's friends. Do it all once and discern what works well for your personality and professional goals. Many marketers I know start their own blog and start out commenting on marketing issues and mixing in some personal stuff as well. This is a great exercise to simply build your writing and critical-thinking skills.

You could go all the way to Rand's Whiteboard series, but that's pretty advanced stuff. Maybe try out some public speaking by getting yourself on a panel at your next American Marketing Association meeting. Panels are great because you get the benefit of being seen and heard without having to carry an entire 30- or 60-minute slot, which terrifies most normal human beings. I speak about 50 times a year but rarely on panels, and I can tell you from experience that you can absolutely up your speaking game (and comfort level) by just doing it— and being so prepared you appear to be off the cuff. Although it's a tough balance to keep, it works for me.

Beyond speaking and content, you need to be thinking about the more subtle aspects of your personal brand. Are you the always-fun person who everybody wants to help succeed? Are you the mad scientist data guru who can quote stats on anything at anytime? Are you the critical-thinking executive who thinks three to four steps ahead, who drives incremental improvements at every level? You need to think deeply about your external persona and how people perceive you; and it'd better be authentic based on your personality, or you'll fail miserably.

I'll share one of my own personal strategies in this realm that I don't think I've ever said out loud to anyone. I frequently think about how certain marketing strategies and tactics apply across all types of companies. For example, I absolutely love it when I see consumer-facing marketers using scoring models to define their most active customers. Those are B2B tactics applied in the B2C realm, and it works like magic. Be thinking beyond the obvious scenarios in front of you, and that will provide a clear gateway to the kind of high-level critical thinking that people value and appreciate.

It's All About the Benjamins

If you've internalized nothing else from this entire book, know that behavioral marketing makes your company more money, and, by extension, it should make *you* more money if you're doing it right. The cart abandon campaigns that convert a $75 average cart-value transaction 22.3 percent of the time is grabbing revenue you never would have seen otherwise. The same thing is true for your lead alert process between the marketing automation platform and your CRM. Triggering an in-person call or visit at the exact right buying moment ups your batting average beyond belief. And translating that success over time into raises and promotions is the part where *you* come in.

On a Benjamins-related side note, you should be prepared for massive pushback from sales as this big behavioral-driven technology stack comes to town. Tracking all their activity is initially going to seem like a pain; but after a couple months sales will realize marketing is now sending them leads that close more often—and within a couple of months, those deals will make up half of their quota. If behavioral marketing can convince a 20-year enterprise sales rep that it works, the sky's truly the limit.

And Finally, Getting Yourself Promoted

I've been around the block in dozens of marketing groups at everything from three-person startups to Fortune 10 companies with hundreds of thousands of employees. The one element you must focus on first is the relationship with your direct manager. Regardless of how many people love you in the organization, or how many want you to work on their team, your direct manager will most often hold your most immediate promotional path in their hands. Spend plenty of time getting to know him or her, and gain a clear understanding of what parameters will be used to measure you. Sounds pretty basic, but you'd be surprised at how many frustrated marketers who vent to me about not being promoted, but can't articulate what they're measured on quarterly and annually.

Beyond a strong personal relationship, it's critical to understand how your skills fit with your manager's core competencies. Are you very similar, and is she the type who needs you to handle the overflow she can't manage? Or is he all about top-line performance and willing to let you run as far as your skill and intelligence will go? Spend the introspective time to develop a deep, honest assessment of your own skills and understand how they complement those around you—both with your direct manager and fellow group members.

And finally, be just as data-driven in your self-assessments as you are in your marketing efforts. Keep a running tally of revenue lift. Track smart decisions that remove cost from a specific part of the business. Look critically at all your work streams, and find a way to quantify every major effort, even if that means inventing a new KPI you can track over time. And be your own greatest advocate while maintaining a running dialogue about your performance all year round. The absolutely worst thing you can do is talk about performance, raises, and promotions only at review times. Be bold and go for it; if you've followed all the tips and thinking in this book, you're miles ahead of the average marketer.

17 Closing Thoughts and the Power of Actions

I hope reading the preceding 16 chapters was enlightening, thought-provoking, and challenged you to think differently about your marketing effort, no matter where you fit in the organizational structure. Almost every marketer I know perpetually exists in the trenches of execution, and rarely has (or makes) the time to ask *why* in any proportion compared to how often they consider *how*. Breaking this cycle could be the single most important takeaway from all these words, and that's my challenge to every reader. Your long-term success won't truly be measured on whether you sent 10 or 12 campaigns this month. The litmus test is more revenue and happier customers.

Every year, I speak at approximately 50 events around the world focused on both new prospects and existing customers, and almost every marketer who attends reports feeling recharged. This is the benefit of being in a room of your peers; the room is full of people who do exactly what you do and who can discuss their own methods and approaches. So find time to network and meet up with other digital marketers in your own town. It serves the dual purpose of getting you off the execution treadmill for an afternoon, and can have an eye-opening effect on your tactics. Just like those one-day events, I trust each of you will take three to four tactics away from this reading, and will implement them in the coming months.

I'll leave you with five very specific takeaways as we wrap up this book:

1. **Get started:** Choose whatever catch phrase you like (everything starts with now; the most difficult step in every journey is the first; ad nauseam) but know there's only one real litmus test after reading this book: Did you implement change? Did you build a new automated program to reach a segment of prospects ready to buy? Will you commit to sharpening your segmentation models to find your least active customers and develop compelling content to win them back? Have you laid out your "next-six" strategy as we discussed in Chapter 5?

    I often talk with our customers about "great being the enemy of good." Don't wait for the perfect customer-buying moment, or until you get one more marketing headcount to get started. Start now and start simply. You can improve your tactics and strategies over time, but erring on the side of action is how you should be thinking right now. Execute on improvements you have direct control over, and be building out a plan around those that require bigger efforts or more organizational coordination. The key is to act.

2. **Be relentless:** Many of the most successful marketers I work with experiment like mad within a constrained subset of their marketing. They nail their top-line approach for key automated programs like

cart abandon or inactive users, and begin almost immediately at the beginning of the queue. They might have eight automated programs that are refreshed and rethought every three to six months, and two more added each quarter.

If this degree of effort seems unachievable, remember that the more you embrace automation and behaviors, the more set-and-forget your marketing becomes. It frees you of the *how* shackles and allows you to spend increasingly more time on the *why*. Initially, you might have to work 25 percent harder, but know that you're making epic progress—both in revenue and customer satisfaction. By approaching your effort with maximum flexibility and an underlying dedication to testing and improvement, your performance will only improve over time.

3. **Focus on revenue:** One of the hallmarks I look for when hiring managers or specialists is an understanding of the bigger picture beyond simply executing great marketing programs. An improvement in email click rates or the percentage of complete records in the database are important interim metrics, but they don't hold a candle to increasing revenue. Sure those actions *improve your opportunity* to drive more revenue, but by themselves they don't fund another headcount or buy more paid media to drive awareness of your solutions.

   So even if you're the newest person on the marketing team, an unrelenting focus on tracking and reporting on revenue lift is critical. At the highest levels of your executive management, that's virtually all they care about. Don't be fooled into grading your own effort on a vanity metric like email-open percentage; the question for every marketer should be how are you contributing to revenue.

4. **Lead the conversation:** Specifically because marketing is undergoing this behavioral-driven transition from batch to highly personalized, the power and spheres of influence are changing rapidly. Today, your business partners likely come to you every fall when

planning for the next fiscal year and outline which products or services will be featured in the marketing. Then, you lay out an annualized calendar. Unfortunately, marketing is too often the order taker and most businesses I see up close could change radically in the space of 12 months.

When we think and act more deeply—and drive our organization to do the same—we earn the right to take a larger role in the planning process. So instead of waiting for the business to ask for a campaign, we're in a position to isolate specific audience subsets that would benefit from a specialized message or offer and proactively start that conversation with the business. The market reality is that the CMO now controls as much (or more) of the technology budget as the CIO does, and that contributes to this reset of roles as well. Marketing is now at the big-kids' table. Make sure you're thinking and acting like you belong there.

5. **Push your team:** For anyone who has direct reports, the challenge to improve your marketing substantially takes on another whole degree of difficulty. It's not just a matter of **you** executing differently, you have to convince, coordinate, and motivate the staff. There are lots of management styles out there, but I find it most effective to combine intense mentoring with elevating expectations.

Simply riding herd on your staff without an absolute commitment to mentoring its youngest members often results in a sweatshop mentality that's counterproductive at best—and alienating to your best employees at its worst. Be prepared to spend time explaining, teaching, and reviewing performance with your direct reports. At the same time, constantly challenge them to improve their performance. Again, there are many methodologies here, but the key is to find one that works well with your personal style. Annual goal planning, some degree of external training, and a recognition program of some sort are all tactics that should be included in your approach.

So let's call this the end of the rah-rah speech. I've given you many tactics and strategies to consider in migrating your marketing effort to be more behavioral. The ball's now squarely in your court. Which two tactics will you have live this month? What relationships will you build to enable holistic improvement over the next 12 months?

If you act, I have succeeded with this book. If you move on to the next title without substantial improvement, I have failed. And failing sucks, so get down to business, my marketing compadres!

INDEX